Kouser,

Thank you for helping me to strengthen my wings!

PATH TO IMPACT

The Rising Leader's Guide
to Growing Smart

I hope you enjoy this book

& that it helps you to broaden your wingspan!

By Wendy Mer....

Wendy

Printed in the United States of America

ISBN: 9781792112492

ABOUT THE AUTHOR

Author, entrepreneur and international speaker Wendy Merrill is committed to helping ambitious Rising Leaders to live more impactful lives at work and beyond. Through her consulting practice, StrategyHorse, Wendy provides entrepreneurs and professionals with the tools they need to understand, define, articulate and convey their individual unique value proposition—the very foundation of growth-oriented leadership. Since 2013, Wendy has been helping aspiring leaders from all over the globe to realize their vision and exceed their goals.

Wendy has had a successful business development career spanning over 23 years. Never a fan of traditional selling or outdated management techniques, she decided early on to approach her career with an eye on the impact she wanted to have with her clients, colleagues and community. By taking a strategic and methodical approach to cultivating and leveraging relationships, Wendy built a rich network of resourceful professionals from all over the world and has helped others do the same.

Known for her candor and straight-talking style, she is a vocal advocate for creative problem solving and has worked with both organizations and early to mid-career professionals to engineer smart growth with an innovative approach to professional development.

Wendy lives near Baltimore, Maryland with her husband, three children and a sassy Beagle. She enjoys mentoring executives and entrepreneurs both in the US and abroad, and currently serves as Board President for the University of Maryland Alumni Association Terp Entrepreneur Network (TEN) and as an advisory board member of the University of Maryland Baltimore County (UMBC)'s Industrial and Organizational Psychology Department. She has also been recognized several times as a leading supporter of women and minorities in business. When she's not working, Wendy enjoys cooking for and being goofy with her family, and when her schedule allows, traveling throughout Italy.

Writing this book has been a dream come true. I am honored not only to be on this journey, but to also continuously learn from all its bends, turns and detours.

I'd like to thank my supportive husband, Stephen, and three babies (even if they're not babies anymore), Emma, Aidan and Noah. I appreciate their patience, cheers and offers to help me write.

A few special words of appreciation go to Rachel Fink and Kelly Brooks-Hailey for lending their time as valued reviewers of my writing, and for their continuous support and words of encouragement.

Heartfelt thanks also go to Karen Singer and Laurie Wasserman for demonstrating the value of having stakeholders in my success.

∼

When the Stars Align and Light the Way,
The Time is Right to Seize the Day.

Contents

Introduction

<u>BREAK THE BOX.</u>

This is not a self-help book.

It's also not a business, management or traditional leadership book. If you are looking for the secret recipe for making millions, buying a speedboat or becoming the next overnight tech bazillionaire, you will likely lose interest in what lies in the pages ahead. There's no shortage of "how to" authors and speakers who have designed their businesses around people's cravings for wealth, popularity and power, but it's just not my thing. I know that loads of people are fiercely loyal to many of the well-known *influencers* whose images are plastered all over social media, bookshelves and Amazon. I'm talking about the folks that have built their empires by penning books with exclamation points in the titles, sharing photos of themselves with famous people or sitting in rare Italian sportscars, and of course, appearing rock star-style in front of sold out crowds of followers.

Don't get me wrong, I'm all about the journey into self-awareness. I just prefer to be a bit more nuanced than my *influencer* comrades. My focus is on creating sustainable change where my presence is no longer needed instead of hooking people on the gateway drug of *The Cult of Wendy*. I wrote this book for professionals who aspire to be impactful both in the workplace and in their communities yet struggle with working out just how to do it. These pages are for the folks that focus on giant seemingly unattainable goals and talk themselves out of taking the first step due to a lack of self-confidence, an undeveloped vision, an inability to effectively self-advocate and/or having no concept of their own individual value proposition.

It's not only about *dreaming big*, it's about figuring out the right way to turn our dreams into realistic and attainable goals –

and then executing our plans. To do this, we must be willing to step out of the box that represents the limitations placed upon us by both ourselves and those around us. *Dreaming big* is not the norm for many people. If you are anything like me, I had to learn *how* to dream, let alone dream *big*. I was not raised to imagine myself as influential in any way, let alone as an agent of change.

Like so many of you, I was raised to fit myself into boxes fashioned by others, no matter how disabling the process might have been. The concept of being a *disruptor,* a coveted title in today's business environment, was frowned upon when I was growing up. When we are conditioned to conform, there's just no room inside our assigned box for *dreaming big*. The desire to do great things is not always about aspiring to breathe the rarified air of the billionaire minority or developing a huge screaming fan base around the globe. It could also lead to effecting social change on a single block in a troubled neighborhood, mentoring a young professional, opening a new business or leading a productive team. Unlike the mantra of so many "self-help gurus", to me, *dreaming big* is about figuring out how to have a productive and positive impact on others, not the sole pursuit of power or monetary wealth.

Growth-oriented developing leaders bear a lot of responsibility in today's business environment. Critical eyes of senior managers are on Millennials and younger Gen X'ers to witness us achieving "the good" we believe ourselves compelled to deliver. What those eyes do not consider is the role we need *them* to play in helping us to make good things happen, and that without their support we are limited in how impactful *we* can be.

To meet the challenge of being a 21st Century Rising Leader, we are obligated to step outside of the confining boxes fashioned for us by our predecessors, parents and peers. We must be unafraid to feel uncomfortable or judged by misinformed peers. We have to learn to celebrate the sharp edges of our square-pegged selves instead of senselessly shaving them down to accommodate the round holes of conformity. We must be able to fiercely advocate for what we need for ourselves as well as what those we lead need from us.

My consulting business was initially created to provide growth-oriented organizations with strategic guidance on how to design and implement effective and efficient business development practices. Firms would hire me to help their younger professionals get better at bringing in new clients. It became apparent that the Baby Boomer executives that retained me were hoping I would provide their younger talent with networking tips and tricks – a "magic pill" approach designed to instantly bring in a flood of new clients. Each time I would meet with a new group of ambitious younger professionals, however, it became clear that their business development struggles stemmed from an absence of leadership skills, both within themselves and among those that signed their paychecks. The C-Suite would demand that their up-and-comers go out and promote the corporate value proposition, and those that were expected to do the promoting often lacked conviction in the very thing they were expected to sell. An organization cannot grow smart or sustainably if the current leaders lack credibility among the presumed future leaders, who in turn have little interest or ability.

The elements of smart growth, such as profitability, client loyalty and low employee turnover are all dependent upon how an organization defines, supports and implements effective leadership. In other words, there is a direct correlation between the business development process and the professional development journey. If we are charged with *making it rain*, we won't be successful unless we know *why* the rain is needed and *how* to inspire others to *keep* it raining. It was precisely this connection that motivated me to graduate from being a transactional salesperson to focus on ways in which I could provide value and inspire others to do the same. Initially I stumbled upon the leadership path, and through a series of daunting challenges and difficult experiences, I was able to define who I was, what I cared about and how I could employ my experience to develop and implement my own *path to impact.*

I wrote this book to help professionals in their 20s, 30s, 40s and beyond, whose idea of success is not defined only in financial terms, but also in the quantifiable impact they want to have in the workplace and community. I've included several anecdotes throughout the book that are based on actual experiences with mostly different names to maintain anonymity. While there is no substitute for the bumps and bruises of real-world experience, my hope is that these chapters provide inspiration, encouragement and the catalyst for ambitious Rising Leaders to do *more,* be *impactful* and champion *smart growth.*

Chapter 1

Learning to Dream BIG

My upbringing was all about fitting in.

Whether it was fulfilling the "traditional" role of a subordinate female in my family, examining my behavior to ensure that I didn't "ruffle feathers" or ensuring that I was always first to blame myself when things didn't go my way, I was conditioned to be fearful of what was *outside of the box.* Even though the restrictive "box" I was raised to inhabit was ill-fitting, the fear of what I might have faced by *not* clipping my own wings was strong enough to keep this square peg stuck in my assigned round hole until the end of my 30s. This meant that I spent most of my young adulthood as a spectator of sorts. I would witness others' success from afar, never imagining myself accomplishing anything of note. The concept of becoming a leader was totally foreign to me. The anxiety of worrying about fulfilling the expectations of those around me consumed me and prevented me from stepping out of my comfort zone, which was actually more like a state of perpetual *discomfort.*

For most of my career, I did not have a mentor. This type of guidance was never offered to me and it didn't occur to me to seek it out for myself until much later. On the contrary, I worked for and with many "anti-mentors" who would often sabotage my professional growth as a means of empowering themselves. Having never worked for a boss with a vested interest in developing my potential, I literally did not know how to do anything outside of my mundane daily grind.

During the first 18 years of my career, I was in various sales roles within the telecom, insurance and financial services industries. In each position I was conditioned to quantify my professional value based on the commissions or bonuses I earned. Even though I found satisfaction in the trusted relationships I had built with clients, to those in charge of managing, motivating and developing me as a professional, I was only worth the sum total of my monthly commission statement. Because of my conditioning and the toxic environments in which I worked, I learned to value myself only based on the revenue that I was directly responsible for. My self-worth was a roller coaster; it ascended dramatically every time I made a sale and plummeted whenever I returned to the office empty handed.

When I was 28, I made the huge decision to join my father's insurance agency. My then-fiancé (now husband) and

I were living in Chicago where I had built a successful insurance practice on my own. We were contemplating getting married and having a family, and we wanted to move closer to my parents in Maryland. Since my dad and I were both in the same field, it seemed to make sense to "join forces" with him and apply my sales ability to growing the family business.

The first year of working with my dad was not as one might imagine. There was no cushy corner office or healthy salary. Instead, I was given a phone and a computer, told that we had little to no marketing budget and that I was responsible for generating my own clients and training myself on the inner workings of the agency. I was charged with building a book of business from scratch for which I would be paid straight commission. If I didn't sell, I didn't earn. Scary, for sure, but as I had experience with this type of compensation in the past, I didn't shy away.

Attracting clients was particularly challenging because we were living in Baltimore, also known as "Smalltimore". As

I was a transplant without the benefit of a local private school education or country club membership, I often had the doors of opportunity slammed in my face. It was cronyism at its finest, and I was an obvious outsider. Fortunately, I knew how to network, a skill I had developed early on, and this was how I set out to feed myself. Gradually, I met a lot of people and broke through many barriers to success. As my network grew over the years, so did my list of clients.

Even though I had worked hard creating a strong local brand for myself, internally I still based my self-worth on how much money I was able to bring into the company. This was particularly challenging because my paycheck never reflected how much time or effort I put into developing a client. Instead, my commissions were always the sum of tiny percentages of whatever insurance premium the client paid (industry standard), reflecting how little control I had over my own income. If a client was only worth $100 or $200 to our agency, I was told to not waste my time regardless of how much they may have needed – and valued – the service I consistently delivered. If I lost a client through no fault of my own because one of the insurance companies screwed up, it didn't matter. I was docked that commission and my value to the agency – and how I saw myself – diminished.

Over time, as I gained experience as a trusted advisor to a variety of businesses, I also acquired valuable knowledge about running a successful enterprise. My father came to rely on my support in the roles of HR, marketing, administration, business development, strategic planning and management. I would often step in where I felt needed, and where my dad lacked interest. Even though I was technically filling 4-5 professional roles within our company, I was still only being compensated based on my sales. My dad would justify not paying me for the other responsibilities by promising me that all my efforts would pay off when the agency would eventually become mine, a few years down the road. I didn't know that I should expect anything more, so I continued to work towards the dangling carrot held in front of me. Eventually I became a partner, but this new title did little to change my compensation.

One day I was fortunate enough to be able to schedule a networking meeting with a very prominent local businessman. It was a big deal to get on his calendar as he was a bit of a local legend. My agenda for the meeting was strictly to secure a place "on his radar" as a possible insurance resource for the large portfolio of businesses he owned, nothing more. His path to success was a rags-to-riches story, and he took great pride in sharing his experiences with me. The meeting lasted for hours and as he asked me questions about the details of how I grew and ran my business it became apparent he was interviewing me.

He eventually came around and asked if I would consider leaving my dad's agency behind to become part of an insurance program he was developing internally. I assumed he meant bringing me on to prospect, sell and build market share in the same type of role I was currently in. I explained to him that I did not see much benefit in making a lateral move. He laughed and said, "Wendy, I don't want you to sell for me. I want you to *build* an insurance company from scratch and *run* the business for me. I want you to be the CEO". My face went pale and I stumbled on my words. I had never thought of myself in this way. This uber-successful businessman saw something in me that I had never seen in myself. Noticing that I was flustered, he told me that I was thinking too small and was allowing my current environment to limit my potential. He then said, "We all have to be able to dream, and if we're going to dream, dream *big*".

His words resonated deeply with me. I spent the entire evening thinking about what he had said and figuring out what *dreaming big* looked like. I eventually decided that if *he* felt I could be the CEO of the agency he wanted to build, I certainly had the skill set to take on this role within a business in which I already had a stake. As I sat down to carefully plan my approach, I felt nervously excited. I reflected upon where the gaps in leadership were within our agency and quantified the opportunity costs associated with not being properly positioned for growth. I diligently researched salary information for similar roles within the region. Most importantly, I carefully considered the reasons why my father should be motivated to allow me to assume this leadership role.

I scheduled a meeting with my dad to present my ideas. One might imagine that a meeting like this would be a cake walk since I was a child asking my father to help me succeed (and in turn help him to do the same). Knowing how proprietary he was about *his* company, I knew this wouldn't be the case, so I made sure I was fully prepared with good information, the willingness to walk if I needed to and a genuine understanding of my worth. My presentation included *why* he needed me to act as CEO, *what* the role looked like and *how* I was qualified. The proposal I put forth included concepts that had been previously foreign to me, especially the part about adding a substantial fixed salary to my fluctuating commission-based compensation plan. For the first time, I was able to understand and articulate my own individual value with confidence and sincerity – and it worked! He actually agreed to my terms and I took over running the agency.

As I formally accepted the new title and compensation plan, it was really just business as usual. I had already been doing much of this job, but I was finally getting fairly paid for it. My professional confidence and approach to life dramatically changed. I suddenly trusted myself more and during my tenure as CEO, I faced – and resolved – enormous challenges that were both emotionally draining and deeply satisfying. As my confidence grew, my intuitiveness sharpened and dramatically shifted my perspective. I began to recognize several sources of toxicity within my work. Negative internal and external factors in the business were threatening my well-being and I started to question what I was doing and why I was doing it.

A useful byproduct of my developing confidence was my quest for *more*. More gratifying work, more professional development, more creativity, more *impact*. It was time to figure out what my mission was and how to apply it in a productive and fulfilling way. When I turned 40, I formed my new business, StrategyHorse Consulting Group. At the same time, I prepared our agency to merge into a larger organization, making sure that my father would be well-situated once I decided to retire from insurance. Later that year, I sold my book of business to another agent, walked away from an 18-year career and began my new journey of *dreaming* – and *doing* big.

Chapter 2

Loose Handcuffs

In 1973 the name *Stockholm Syndrome* was invented to describe a condition whereby hostages involved with a bank robbery in Stockholm developed an emotional connection with their captors. Sufferers of Stockholm Syndrome believe in the humanity of their captors and therefore feel sympathy and trust towards them instead of condemning their predatory and dangerous behavior. This condition is not only found in the world of kidnapping and crime but is distressingly common in the workforce as well.

In the business world Stockholm Syndrome victims are subordinates that question their own abilities, efforts and overall value in order to satisfy the perceived goals of their superiors. Over the years, I've encountered so many bright professionals who convince themselves that their toxic work environment is not *that* bad. They tend to think that somehow their hard work will be rewarded despite the apathy of their managers, or that a moderate amount of abuse in the office is considered normal and therefore acceptable. It's easy for me to recognize people who struggle as victims of Stockholm Syndrome because I too suffered in the same way for the majority of my career. If we learn to recognize how this condition manifests itself in our daily work experiences, we will be able to vastly improve our office environments and *paths to impact.*

It's the 32-year old marketing director with the predatory boss that calls her "pretty young thing" in front of clients and colleagues, who sticks around because she feels she's overpaid for what she does. It's the 38-year old CPA who puts forth an exceptional effort to qualify for a partnership position only to be turned down by a senior partner whose ego is threatened by the fact that his clients value his younger counterpart more than they do him. It's the 41-year old non-profit board member whose efforts are sabotaged by the board president to maximize her individual power within the organization they serve. And of course, it was yours truly, a 38-year old insurance agent wearing six hats of responsibility, getting paid for only one and never questioning the rationale behind it. Each one of these examples shows a Rising Leader who is held *captive* by the belief that they couldn't possibly deserve better than what they've been offered.

Each of these professionals aspires to be successful, yet they've allowed themselves to be handcuffed to a destructive situation. We frequently make the damaging assumption that our supervisors have *our* best interests at heart instead of their own selfish needs. While we may *feel* stuck in our shackles, the reality is that the handcuffs are actually quite loose and the only thing keeping us from slipping our hands out to embrace freedom is our inability to recognize those thwarting our *path to impact*. We can all unshackle ourselves from detrimental work situations, but the key to freedom lies in our ability to understand the differences between our goals and our supervisors' true intentions.

Even though you'll find examples of WSS (workplace Stockholm Syndrome) in many different fields, I've seen the most extreme cases within the most educated groups of professionals. It seems that the higher up one is on the advance-degreed food chain, the more likely insecurity-induced narcissism is in play. In fact, I'd argue that the foundation of most successful law firms, healthcare establishments and even academia is based on manipulative behavior that flows from management down to administrative staff. Why are these environments such fertile ground for this type of predatory behavior? Probably because those that feel pressure to be the smartest guy or gal in the room possess surprisingly fragile egos, making them especially vulnerable to being taken advantage of.

MICHAEL

A small group of lawyers who were partners in a large national firm had invited me to work with them to help their budding practice group reach its full growth potential. These attorneys were super smart and enjoyed an impeccable reputation within their niche practice area. The firm prided itself on being innovative and the leadership was vocal about their interest in supporting the professional development of their attorneys, something that seemed to set them apart from some competitors – at least on the surface.

The youngest partner in the group and I had built a great rapport. Michael had an exceptionally polished executive presence, outstanding communication skills and a top-notch education. The partners requested a proposal from me and initially explained that they had the authority to sign off on such a project. It turned out they did not have the power to greenlight our project after all, and my proposal landed under a

34

pile on their marketing department's desk. The firm dragged their feet for months, much to the frustration of the group that originally invited me in. Even though the proposed engagement was requested by this highly profitable practice group, the firm decided not to hire me. Once I heard the news, I had a candid conversation with Michael to understand why the firm decided not to invest in our project. During our phone call, his frustration was clear.

He vented about the irrational decision process that determined not only the outcome of our potential project, but other critical growth opportunities for his group as well. In a moment of candor, he told me that he recently had offers from other firms for double his salary and a much healthier marketing budget. So, I asked him the obvious question: why did he stay? At first, he was quiet and then he responded in a shaky voice, "I don't know...that's a good question." A year later, I tried to follow up with Michael to see how he was doing and found he was still at the same firm and in the same position. He had stopped returning my calls and according to my research, his group's positioning in the marketplace was relatively unchanged.

I've encountered countless *Michaels* both in my professional and personal life, and as I explained earlier, I've also walked many miles in the very same shoes. There are loads of *Michaels* in non-profits, accounting concerns, engineering firms, consulting practices, healthcare institutions, government agencies and…the list goes on. So many ambitious and enterprising people willingly exchange their dreams and their pride for a false sense of security. I say "false" because as safe as a steady paycheck and a predictable routine may seem, they can present far more risk than may meet the eye. The risk that complacency presents to Rising Leaders is the threat it poses to our ability to make an impact. If we aspire to reach our full potential and have a positive and lasting effect on others, we are destined to fail if we limit our thinking about how we *can* and *should* be creating the difference we want to see in the workplace and in the world.

The name of the game for any business is growth, and it's no secret that companies need structure and personnel that fit into a strategic hierarchy to realize their goals. These organizational charts become problematic when those involved do not take the time to understand:

1) Their own motivation, 2) The motivation of their colleagues and 3) How to align everyone's motivation to accomplish a common goal.

MELISSA

This absence of synergy is particularly common in larger organizations. Melissa was an engineer in a national firm and was considered a "rising star" among her peers. Her commitment to the success of the firm was matched only by her stellar work ethic. She was the youngest partner by about 15 years, and her colleagues were set in their ways and reticent to embrace any change to management style or growth strategy.

Unsurprisingly, Melissa's concerns about the future of the firm fell on mostly deaf ears as most of her partners were biding their time until retirement. She was a good manager and saw first-hand the concerns and challenges of her employees, but when she brought them to the partnership table to determine solutions, her ideas were accounted for but not implemented. Instead of taking a step back to consider what her partners really cared about, Melissa charged forward, putting more and more responsibility on her plate to effect necessary change.

She was tired of her colleague's apathy and figured that she should take it upon herself to remedy whatever needed to be fixed within the company (a common practice of many Rising Leaders). Her partners were thrilled that Melissa was taking this initiative because it meant that they didn't have to do it *and* they didn't need to pay anyone else to do what she was willing to do *for free*.

No matter how hard Melissa worked, not much changed. Her partners handed her a few pats on the back here and there, but their kind words only amounted to lip service. At first, the compliments abated some of her frustrations, but after a while, it became apparent to Melissa that she was exhausting herself and failing to make headway in terms of the change she aspired to create. Had she seriously considered her partners' motivations and unwillingness to exert themselves *before* she set out on her solitary expedition to cure her company's ills, she would have understood that they were *never* going to support or implement her solutions because of the threat posed to the other partners' collective comfort level.

Eventually, Melissa saw the writing on the wall. It took many months of 70-hour workweeks to realize that her efforts were in vain. She finally decided to cut her losses and apply her skills on behalf of another firm, this time with a smaller and younger group of partners. A few years later, her old company was hemorrhaging talent. Meanwhile, Melissa was thriving at her new firm. She was able to eventually slip out of the handcuffs she thought kept her at her old firm and she was now empowered to invest in strategic growth efforts, including successful business development and recruiting campaigns. She spent years trying to convince her *partner-captors* to unlock her cuffs before she realized that she alone possessed the ability to free herself.

As Rising Leaders, we must understand how our choices mold our ability to be effective and impactful. It is critical for us to take the time to comprehend whether or not our value proposition is sincerely aligned with our employer's objectives. For this, we must be self-aware and comprehend what drives us and *why*.

The Holy Trinity of WHY

As I mentioned, we cannot hope to be impactful unless we are able to lay bare our true motivation. If we are only aware of *what* intrigues us and not *why* it captures our interest, we will only be partially successful. It's not just about articulating *our* WHY, but also interpreting the motivation of *others* as well. Self-awareness is not only the cornerstone of leadership, it is also essential to any successful business development initiative. To understand *how* we can provide value to others we must first try and figure out *why* we want to be of value. This is a big, abstract concept and can be overwhelming to think about. I have developed a simple way of drilling down our various layers of motivation so we can effectively employ them in our quest to be more impactful. I call it the *Holy Trinity of Why*.

The Holy Trinity of *Why*

1. What do you care about?

2. What do you fear?

3. What do you want?

What do you care about?

This question pertains to anything and everything. It's not just about what drives you professionally, it's also about whatever keeps you up at night or what may bring a tear to your eye. For those of us that don't work for a mission-driven non-profit, we are trained to remove emotion from what we do. Instead, we are pressured to become technicians geared towards providing sound deliverables that give us a competitive edge. Many of us are trained to limit our thinking to whatever pre-fabricated box our managers have established for us, and when we do this, we lose sight of the meaning behind what we do. The *why* gets eclipsed by the *what*.

The pressure to perfect technical skills distracts us from discovering our individual value proposition, which should go way beyond technical expertise. Our value prop. should embody every way in which we contribute to the overall growth of our organizations. If we don't allow ourselves to ponder what we care about, we will never understand – and convey – how our passion to help others, our insatiable curiosity, or our need to make decent money plays a significant role in growing the collective bottom line. It's not just about believing in what we do on the job, it's also understanding what we deeply care about on a personal level.

Recently I was retained by a non-profit organization to help their Rising Leaders feel more engaged and productive. Two of the program participants, Tim and Rob, worked together closely, one supervising the other. They built a great rapport and deeply respected one another. After speaking with each one individually, however, it was apparent that neither guy had any idea of what motivated the other. In coaching Tim, I discovered that his dream was to provide a much better life for his daughter than what he had experienced as a child. He had suffered many financial hardships growing up and he worked long hours to protect his child from the same unfortunate circumstances. When he talked about his daughter, his face lit up. It was clear what Tim cared about and how it drove him to work hard every day.

When it was time for me to work with Tim's supervisor Rob, our session revealed his frustration with high employee turnover on his team. We spoke at length about the challenges he faced holding on to people and we both agreed that Tim was his "rising star". Rob expressed worry that Tim may also consider leaving at some point and I asked him if he knew what motivated his best employee. He shook his head. I asked Rob if he ever sat down to speak with Tim about what was most important to him, and more specifically, how he could help him to reach his goals. He hadn't. I shared my conversation with Tim about his commitment to providing his daughter with a good life and how he was willing to do whatever it took to ensure her success. Rob looked pensive. He knew that Tim had a daughter, but it never occurred to him that there might be a connection between Tim's family life and his work ethic.

As Rob was working with me to strengthen his leadership skills and improve his ability to engage and inspire his team, I suggested to him that if he were mindful of what Tim's motivation was, it would be easier for him to figure out how to help his best guy realize his own definition of success. If Tim were to feel supported and personally invested in by his manager, not only would he stick around, but he would likely take a vested interest in recruiting and retaining his colleagues, thus helping Rob with *his* biggest challenge.

What do you fear?

I believe that fear drives everything we do. The fear of failure drives us to work harder and study more. The fear of being alone drives us to enter the dating scene to seek out a partner. The fear of injury or death makes us employ certain safety measures in our lives. We all carry our fears around with us, but how many of us have ever taken inventory of them in an attempt to understand them and work through what scares us? Just as being able to articulate what we care about is essential to our personal and professional growth, if we don't wrap our minds around what's holding us back, we will never be impactful leaders.

Everyone harbors some kind of fear that imprisons us in some way, and I've found that when we own up to what concerns us most, and do so publicly (with discretion), we are exponentially more effective in inspiring others to meaningful action. This is because *fear is human* and when we own our vulnerabilities it makes us *relatable*. Relatability is the gateway to trust, and the consumers, clients and employees of the future will demand that their needs be met by providers who can genuinely relate to them.

FAILURE

Success is its own reward, but failure is a great teacher too, and not to be feared.
— Sonia Sotomayor

I do a lot of work with Millennials, both coaching younger professionals as well as advising their more seasoned supervisors on how to embrace their younger workforce and client base. I take particular pleasure in debunking so many of the myths that Baby Boomers and some Gen-Xers enjoy promoting about their younger colleagues. I've worked with hundreds of people under the age of 40 and they are some of the hardest workers I've ever encountered, a far cry from the "lazy and entitled" labels that the media likes to throw around. The Millennials I know are passionate and driven to play a part of something larger than them, something important, something *impactful*. Present any 28, 32 or 38-year old with a meaty corporate mission, a committed team with which to collaborate, and a specific execution plan, and the 40-hour workweek is thrown out the window.

It's not a poor work ethic or lack of responsibility that prevents younger professionals from dreaming and doing *big*, it's a paralyzing fear of failure. Most younger folks in the workforce were raised with smartphones from a very early age. This technology provided constant access to instant information and empowered those on the younger end of the spectrum to evade failure. As a member of Generation X, my friends and I were raised to embrace the *school of hard knocks* mentality. Many of us were managed through fear and taught to manage others much in the same way. We understood that mistakes, disappointments and failures were inevitable. Of course, the disappointments were no fun to endure at the time, but we understood (even if a bit later on) that the bumps and bruises we may have suffered along our professional development paths were necessary for eventually realizing success.

In fact, technology has made many of my younger colleagues into *veal*, confining them to failure-proof pens, much like how baby cows are raised to minimize muscle development and preserve their tender meat. They have been prevented from developing the "muscle mass" that comes from taking risks, experiencing failure and moving forward in a more prudent way. Developing this *muscle* by overcoming failure is essential for anyone with big goals and high aspirations. In addition, understanding this prevalent fear of failure is critical for Rising Leaders who want to be impactful and are committed to inspiring others to do the same. In the absence of failure there can be no success. After all, how will we recognize what real success looks or feels like without being able to sense its absence?

LOOKING STUPID

He who asks a question is a fool for five minutes; he who does not ask a question remains a fool forever. -Chinese Proverb

When I was in college, I applied to an exclusive summer internship program at one of my favorite art museums. As an Art History major, I was thrilled to have been selected to provide support to one of their most well-known curators. At first, the opportunity really boosted my ego, which was paper-thin at the time. At 19 years old, I had no idea what my career path would look like, and I was interested in the internship program as a valuable learning opportunity to complement my liberal arts education. I was also excited for the opportunity to use my newly-acquired Italian language skills, which were critical to the work I was to be doing.

As most internships were in the early 1990s, it was an unpaid summer job and it required me to find an apartment nearby and cover my own expenses for the entirety of the program. On my first day of work, my new boss, Dr. M. as I'll call her, gave me an icy reception. Her cold aloofness preyed on my massive insecurities and made me keenly aware of the fact that I was the least experienced student in the program. The other interns were all graduate students and for most of them, this was their 2nd or 3rd internship.

On the second day, Dr. M. gave my fellow interns and I directions – orders really – as to what we were to do. Her directions included the use of the word "monograph", a term I had never heard before. As I was keen to succeed, I asked her to explain what the word meant. There was a deafening silence. Disgusted, she stared at me and proceeded to berate me in front of two other interns for my "limited vocabulary." She spent what seemed like 5 minutes chastising me for "not knowing anything" and asked me if I had learned anything at all at my university. It took every bit of strength for me to not crumble into tears. I accepted the lashing and internalized what she had said. I spent the rest of the summer desperate for a kind word from her. It never came.

In the early 90s, interns would usually agree to accept a recommendation letter in lieu of compensation for their contributions. When I reached out to Dr. M. with what I thought was a normal request for such a letter, her response flattened me. She told me that she *might* be willing to write a letter on my behalf, but "it would all depend on who would read it". She proceeded to explain, "If you wanted to apply to Harvard or Yale for graduate school, I'd be unwilling to recommend you. If there is something else you had in mind, do let me know". I had never been made to feel so small, so stupid or so inferior in my life. Here was this world-renowned academic telling me that I was worthless in her view. I returned to school that fall with my tail tucked between my legs and any tiny bit of self-confidence I had worked so hard to amass had all but disappeared.

The following summer I decided to put myself *out there* again and apply to another internship program, this time at my favorite museum, The Metropolitan Museum of Art in New York. I was cautiously excited when I realized that I was qualified to apply to the program. I was able to fill each of their requirements, and then some. I had a nice recommendation letter from a professor who believed in me, and the Met was willing to pay a decent stipend to those that were accepted. I anxiously awaited their response, and when it arrived, my heart sank. My application was rejected, and I found out later that my candidacy was sabotaged by Dr. M.

My internship experience with Dr. M. scarred me for many, many years. Even though I was consistently on the Dean's List throughout college, I didn't feel intellectually competent until decades later. She instilled in me a deep fear of appearing stupid in front of others and it cast a shadow on me that I felt in every job I held for over

20 years. It wasn't until I learned to embrace my insatiable curiosity as a strength that I finally felt confident enough to step into the ring with just about anyone. Once I felt comfortable with soliciting help when I needed it, I was able to engage with people in a different way. Instead of being judged negatively, people ended up trusting me *more.* They confided in me and welcomed me as a stakeholder in their success. Why? Because I was human, just like them, and my imperfections and vulnerabilities made me less threatening and more relatable, empowering me to be more impactful.

OWNING YOUR POWER

Even though many of us *think* that we aspire to leadership positions at work and in our communities, when we are presented with the opportunity to fully understand and apply our potential, we freeze. We become severely limited by our fear of realizing just *what we can do* and then owning the responsibility of *actually doing it*. Some may call this a fear of success, but really, it's being scared of creating favorable circumstances for ourselves instead of expecting others to hand us the opportunity to prove ourselves.

One way we can overcome this fear is to focus less on the quantifiable outcomes of our efforts and more on what it feels like to conquer our internal scaredy-cats. The path to becoming a savvy and effective leader is just as important, if not more so, than the end result. Each time we are faced with a challenge, we must celebrate when we are able to dig our heels in. On the other hand, we must also pay close attention to when fear gets the best of us, so we can learn from the experience and move forward towards becoming the impactful leaders we want to be.

What do you want?

This question seems so simple, but it's actually one of the most profound things we can ask ourselves. This is probably why so few of us allow ourselves to ponder what our pot of gold looks like. Instead, we blindly trust that the rainbow will inevitably lead us there with little to no input from us. If we are not able to articulate what we want as individuals, how can we be the leaders that spark others to have a meaningful impact both in the workplace and community?

Instead of carving out the time to carefully consider what we want for ourselves and those that are important to us, we spend more time pondering what *others* want *for* us – and *from* us. It almost feels indulgent to define what we want, as if it is somehow selfish to take ownership of our lives and the impact we want to have. Being direct about where we want to be is not at all selfish. In fact, I would argue that clearly expressing our goals and the processes we will employ to achieve what we want is actually complementary to and a requirement of effective leadership.

When I started my consulting business, I knew I wanted to follow a different path than that of my earlier career. I wanted to be happy and feel good about the work I was doing. In the beginning, this was as specific as I could get. I worked really hard and was always driven by my desire to be impactful and disrupt the status quo, however, I never sat down with myself – or my husband – to discuss or define what we wanted or how my new business would contribute to the success of our family. The first time we did this was not until my fifth year in business, after a close advisor recommended we do so. It was some of the greatest advice I have ever received. I suddenly gave myself the permission to put a fine point on what I really wanted, and once my husband and I made the time to communicate with one another, I was able to define my goals. This allowed me to take the necessary steps to make a difference in the lives of my family members, with my clients and in the community as a whole.

The T-Chart

Thinking about what we want is not easy. Defining our path can be so overwhelming that we tend to distract ourselves by focusing on safe tasks instead of pursuing the life we crave. Sometimes the simplest processes yield the most fruit, and when a Rising Leader needs to decide how to pursue their destiny, I've found there's no better tool than the old-fashioned "T-Chart". I was first introduced to this exercise by a friend, just as I was considering making my big career change. In fact, my T-Chart results kicked off my campaign to start StrategyHorse.

Grab a sheet of paper & draw a giant "T" down the middle. On the left side, list everything you hate to do & never want to do again. On the right side, list everything you love to do.

Don't hold back and don't overlook the small stuff. No one is going to read this but you.

Once you reach the bottom of your chart you will have your answer, or at least a strong indication of how you should chart your course for success.

Chapter 3

<u>Value</u>

The transfer of value is the cornerstone of every business transaction, partnership, friendship, romantic relationship, religious affiliation and educational experience. We often get so distracted by our desire to succeed that we forget *why* we entered into a particular relationship or transaction in the first place. Think about the last partnership (personal or professional) in which you have participated. When you entered into the relationship, did you have a clear expectation of what you hoped to accomplish in your role? What about your expectations of your partner? Was the reciprocal exchange of value ever discussed or documented? If we want to be impactful, we must possess the ability to appraise and convey not only the value we expect from others, but of our own individual unique value.

Sounds simple and obvious, right? The truth is, most of us struggle mightily with understanding, quantifying and promoting the value we provide to others. As I mentioned earlier, many of us tend to focus on fitting ourselves into boxes that others have fashioned for us. When we interview for jobs, our salary requirements usually have little to do with the ROI we will provide to our prospective employer. Instead, we imagine ourselves with a price tag that mirrors every other candidate that has a similar education or the same number of years of experience. If we fail to comprehend the real tangible value we provide to our employers, colleagues and clients, we will continuously fall short of achieving our objectives.

CONFIDENCE IS NOT ARROGANCE

Tracy was looking to change jobs and a mutual friend recommended that we meet, thinking that I might have some ideas for her. Tracy had 10 years of professional experience and was at a career crossroads. When I asked her what she was looking for she responded with an ambivalent shrug. She began reciting her resume, listing her titles and employers, but didn't mention anything about what she had accomplished or where she was headed. I wanted to help her, but without an idea of where she wanted to land, I wasn't going to be able to make any suggestions or introductions. I asked her to tell me what her skills were, to share what she was really good at. She said, "Well, I don't want to seem stuck-up or arrogant, but I've had several people tell me that I am a good manager". And there it was, an apology for owning her value. I've heard versions of this statement more often than I can count, and candidly, sometimes it's been from my own mouth.

So many Rising Leaders minimize our accomplishments for fear of being judged by others as having some overinflated sense of self. But confidence *is not* arrogance as long as it's based on a legitimate track record of accomplishments. This is an example of "imposter syndrome", as it's been called, and contrary to popular belief, it is not limited to just women and younger professionals. Rising Leaders at both the early *and* mid-stage career level struggle with quantifying and promoting their talents. Defining an individual value proposition is even more challenging for those of us that were raised to conform to others' expectations, and we need to be willing to see ourselves objectively and lose the fear of thinking big.

BUILDING BIG THINKING

To facilitate this process, I've created some simple exercises designed to channel skills, interests and emotions to reveal what each of us brings to the table. Throughout this book, you will see seven activities that have been designed for both individuals and teams. I encourage you to take the time not only to do these for yourself, but to share both the exercises and results with your colleagues and direct reports. To truly benefit from these exercises, it's not enough to do them once. Because our lives, dreams and situations are fluid, I recommend revisiting each at least once a year, preferably more.

Exercise 1:
CHALLENGE/SOLUTION/RESOURCE CHART

On a whiteboard or piece of paper, draw 3 columns with a title row at the top that reads: "Challenge, Solution, Resources".

In the 1st column, list a few challenges that you'd like to solve. They may be personal or professional in nature.

In the 2nd column, write down the solutions you aspire to. If you end up leaving this space blank it's OK as this is not the most important part of the exercise.

Moving on to the 3rd column, this is where you should list any resources available to you that will help you arrive at & deliver a sound solution.

Example 1.

Challenge	Solution	Resources
I need better childcare.	Find a reliable nanny or babysitter.	Computer, internet, social media, recommendations from colleagues, advice from other parents
I'd like to take on a leadership position at work.	?	Advice from mentors, colleagues, supervisors, books/courses on leadership, online resources, coaches, etc.
I want to attract better candidates for job openings.	Advertise open positions in the places where I'm most likely to find qualified and ambitious professionals.	Internet, social media, professional peer groups, professional community online forums, networking, job sites, career centers

Exercise 2:

WHAT'S YOUR UNIQUE INDIVIDUAL VALUE PROPOSITION?

On your whiteboard/paper write down the following categories:

FRIENDS/FAMILY

COMPANY

CLIENTS

COLLEAGUES/DEPARTMENT

PROFESSIONAL COMMUNITY (INDUSTRY PEERS)

SOCIAL COMMUNITY (NEIGHBORHOOD, RELIGIOUS AFFILIATIONS, CIVIC INVOLVEMENT)

Think about your role within each category and define the value you believe you provide to each.

What words come to mind?

The most common descriptions I've received over the years are: *reliable, responsible, trustworthy, team player and honest.* These are all admirable qualities that engender trust and invite opportunities, however, they are **adjectives**, *not* **values**. To define our value, we must understand what being reliable, responsible, trustworthy, etc. *does* for the people in each category. *In other words, how does our being responsible affect our family and friends?* For those of us aspiring to be impactful leaders, we must first position ourselves as *Trusted Advisors.*

It doesn't matter if you are a supervisor at a manufacturing plant, a member of a non-profit board or a technology entrepreneur, the foundation upon which effective leadership is built is the ability to be seen as *Trusted Advisors* by doing two simple things for others:

Reducing or alleviating stress

&/or

Saving or making them money

If we incorporate this lens into every endeavor, we will always deliver value. One of the greatest things we can do as leaders is help others regain control by addressing and overcoming fear. Remember, fear drives almost everything we do, and if someone is willing and able to help mitigate what scares us it will always reduce our stress and ultimately put money in our pockets.

This rings particularly true for professional services practitioners, specifically anyone who bills for their time. I do a lot of work with attorneys, accountants, engineers and consultants and I've never met a professional who can provide a clear explanation of how their hourly rate is determined. It doesn't matter if it is a young CPA charging $125 an hour or a senior level mergers and acquisitions lawyer whose hourly rate hovers around $1000. If someone cannot account for *why* they charge what they do, how is a client expected to comprehend what they're getting for their investment? As Artificial Intelligence begins to pose a real threat to those of us in the advisory business, it's never been more important to recognize and convey the comprehensive value we bring to our clients. This requires us to go above and beyond providing standard technical advice while we are on the clock.

Instead, we must constantly seek ways in which we demonstrate to our clients the vested interest we have in helping them reach their goals. Maybe a strategic introduction or the sharing of an idea. This way of thinking has traditionally been thought of as a *value-added* approach, sort of like a bag of potato chips with a fluorescent orange "Bonus Bag – 30% more chips!" label on it. Impactful leaders account for these efforts as an *inherent part* of their value proposition, not as something that was added as a gimmicky afterthought. Understanding and appreciating the full value we provide to our clients can be tricky. This third exercise was designed to help the billable crowd, but I've also found it to be useful for other businesspeople who might be struggling with determining their pricing.

Exercise 3:

DISSECTING THE RATE

Draw a rectangle with several vertical "slices" in it. Then write your hourly rate or project fee at the very top.

Next, in each "slice" write all the things that your rate includes, from the most obvious on the left to the least obvious on the right. It will probably be difficult to get past experience, education & overhead, but keep going.

Once you've filled in as many components as you can, assign a percentage to each.

$200

Experience	Education	Overhead	Industry Expertise	Staff	Network
20%	10%	20%	15%	15%	30%

If you're questioning my math, the total *is* actually 110%, to illustrate the fact that we should always go above and beyond to provide additional value to our clients. Notice what's missing? No mention at all of the "going market rate". This is because one's value should never be determined by what others are charging. The last slice on the right attributes the highest value to the curation of a strategic network. The more qualified introductions you can make on behalf of your client, the better. This is not only how you provide value, but also how you create a lasting impact as well as fierce loyalty.

Those on the job hunt also benefit from measuring and accurately presenting their value. No matter what kind of position you might be interviewing for, there's one thing I can absolutely guarantee: the person across the table from you wants to know how you can make them/their team/their organization more money.

~

Salespeople are decent at gearing their responses to address this challenge, but if you are a graphic designer, engineer or outreach coordinator for a community foundation, you are likely not thinking about how you will quantify your value in this way. Even if you are not in a direct revenue generating position, your contribution to the organization must exceed your overall compensation package. If you are applying to be a marketing manager, think specifically about how your creativity, intuitive ability and project management skills will complement your employer's growth objectives. If you aspire to a leadership position within a non-profit, it's all about the continuous development of stakeholders in the organization's mission. And if you seek a decent salary, you must be prepared to share a detailed plan of how you will generate a legitimately better outcome for the organization's beneficiaries as well as its staff.

What about entrepreneurs? We are definitely not exempt from the need to polish our interviewing skills, we just need to tweak them to appeal to a different audience. The biggest struggle for entrepreneurs is to verbalize how the "wow factor" and passion behind our businesses will directly translate into real gains for potential investors, clients and employees. This is why it is so important for those starting and running businesses to quantify and convey their unique value as leaders, so they can convince others of how that value will impact both staff productivity and market share.

Chapter 4

Selfie-**Advocacy**

WHAT'S A PERSONAL BRAND & WHY DO I NEED ONE?

If you google the phrase *Personal Branding*, the results will include training materials, millions of articles, books and a few unfortunate references to the Kardashians. The concept of branding oneself is relatively new in the mainstream business world, and a lot of Rising Leaders struggle with *who they are* publicly.

The simplest way to understand branding is to think of wine tasting. For those of us who enjoy wine, a big part of the tasting process is examining the *finish*, which is just a fancy word for aftertaste.

When you sip a wine, the finish is what determines whether you take another sip, buy a glass, a bottle, a case, or just spit it out into a big silver bucket. A brand is like the finish of a wine, it's an impression that compels someone to learn more about one's value proposition, engage a service or buy a product, refer their friends and family or just walk away. Rising Leaders must be intentional about understanding, defining and promoting their personal brand if they want to be impactful. Thoughtful personal branding is critical to how colleagues, clients, and the community perceive our value. Impact-oriented professionals should aspire to brand themselves in one of three ways:

- *Thought Leader*
- *Center of Impact*
- *Combination of Both*

Many moons ago when I was building my insurance practice, I faced a lot of challenges. The business I was in had very few barriers to entry (who doesn't know an insurance agent) and what I was selling was highly commoditized. I also had no network at the time and no idea about who I should be selling to. I was sure of one thing, though. I knew that I had to provide something of value to the community *in addition* to procuring insurance coverage for them. I set out to position myself as a Center of Impact (COI), making thoughtful connections intended to help local professionals succeed and businesses to grow. I didn't realize it at the time, but the COI role I aspired to was actually my *personal brand* in the making. But becoming a valuable resource in the local business community was not easy.

I was obviously not part of the *Old Boy Network,* and I had just moved to Baltimore knowing no one outside of immediate family. I figured that if I met a lot of people and tried to surround myself with experienced professionals who knew more than me, I would eventually establish the bench of resources I needed to enjoy a bona fide COI reputation. My marketing dollars were extremely limited, so I had to figure out ways to build out my network on a tiny budget.

Over time, I got to know a lot of people and I was eventually able to focus on *curating* my network, instead of *collecting* it. Whenever I'd attend a coffee meeting with a new contact I would spend the entire time learning about them and the challenges they faced, listening for ways in which I could help them. These conversations *rarely ever* included insurance, yet most of them led to new clients and referral sources for me. A few years into my "personal branding campaign", I began to receive calls from various business owners and professionals asking for advice, ideas and referrals to qualified resources. This was when I knew that I was finally delivering *value* as a *Trusted Advisor*, and this was how I differentiated myself from my competitors, most of whom had distinct advantages over me.

BECOMING A COI

Becoming a *Center of Impact* is not for everyone. Sure, there are plenty of professionals who frequent the local networking scene and fancy themselves to be "thoughtful connectors" but doing so does not necessarily merit the label. As a seasoned and shrewd networker, I've encountered lots of people who proclaim their fabulous connecting talents to whomever is willing to accept their business card or LinkedIn invitation.

The difference between those that set colleagues up on random "professional blind dates" and someone who's all about making good things happen is *motivation*. If you want to earn a reputation as a premier COI, it's all about possessing a generous spirit, and a genuine interest in helping *others* to reach their goals. As COI's, our mission should be to deliver continuous value to our network through emotive investment. We must genuinely care about facilitating the success of others. If we create strategic and thoughtful introductions between people whose values are aligned, we will be far more impactful than we imagined possible.

ARE YOU A THOUGHT LEADER?

For those of us who prefer to be impactful by positioning ourselves as a valuable source of information, becoming a *go-to* resource for a particular subject is smart branding. Being a thought leader is consistent with our *Trusted Advisor* goals of minimizing stress and saving/making money because providing an education will always ease the fear and expense of ignorance. The successful promotion of oneself as a thought leader is about getting others to see you as a subject matter expert. This requires not only knowledge, but also a carefully choreographed plan for how you will promote your knowledge (events, speaking, writing, teaching, membership in industry-specific associations). This is an ideal brand for people who are more introverted and less likely to take the initiative to proactively contribute to the networks of others.

THE BRANDING OF TONY

Tony was trying to build his commercial real estate business. As a broker, he derived his income from commissions generated by buying and selling properties for his clients. A tough gig, to be sure, made even tougher by stiff competitors with long-standing relationships, deeper marketing pockets and more experience. Tony was determined to carve a niche for himself and engaged me to help him differentiate his business from other brokers. Before getting his real estate license, Tony spent 10 years working for his family's business. He worked closely with his parents and siblings to perpetuate a legacy spanning over 100 years. As most family business *veterans* will tell you, working with relatives is never what it's cracked up to be. In fact, the stresses and struggles of multi-generational enterprises have created an affinity group of sorts, where members form and share an instantaneous and unique bond with one another.

Back when I was working with my father, whenever I would encounter a professional who was working with or for family members, this shared experience immediately engendered trust. So, when I was helping Tony to define his target market, we decided it made sense for him to become an advisor to family businesses looking to make real estate investments. Because of his background, he already enjoyed credibility within his peer group. He understood that businesses preparing to make large real estate purchases needed a *Trusted Advisor* to minimize their risk and guide them through the process. Who better to do so than a fellow family business veteran?

To establish himself as a thought leader, Tony was intentional about his business development and marketing efforts. He consistently posted articles on social media about various topics pertaining to family businesses, he landed speaking engagements where he reached audiences that included both family businesses and other professionals working to advise them, he started a family business-centric study group to discuss best practices and he strategically networked with other advisors supporting clients with blood relations on the payroll. Tony became known as *the family business broker,* and over time, generated a robust referral network and loyal clients. In addition to creating a successful business model, Tony's thought leadership impact spread to a larger scale when he joined a national family business roundtable and became a regular contributor to a national family business journal. His insights regarding the real estate needs of businesses affected by family dynamics have helped members of this unique community across the country.

THE IMPORTANCE OF EXECUTIVE PRESENCE

When I entered the job market in 1994, printed resumés were a really big deal. I remember going to the stationery store and spending a long time deciding between various types of fancy stock paper,

84

and then heading home to carefully place each expensive sheet into the snail-paced printer to prepare for a job interview. My friends and I would spend hours painstakingly squeezing every word onto one page (2 pages were a huge no-no) and proofreading the lines 150-200 times before placing these valuable documents in our fancy leather portfolios.

As we were preparing to graduate from college, we all went shopping with our moms to buy an "interview suit" that was either navy blue or black and was accompanied by a silk blouse, pantyhose and pumps with heels that were under 1.5". When we arrived suited up for our interviews, we were greeted by our potential employers with firm handshakes and trick questions designed to trip up our well-rehearsed routine. There was an official start, middle and end to each interview, with a standard follow-up practice that included formal letters thanking our interviewers with fancy wording and envelopes with typed addresses. Once we were eventually hired, we were conscious of our every move, anxious to fit the company mold by paying careful attention to each work outfit (skirts were at the knee), the firmness of our handshakes, how we spoke to our supervisors and the schedule we were expected to follow.

Regardless of whether we were receptionists, assistants, coordinators or junior salespeople, young people entering the 9-5 workforce were expected to follow very specific protocols. Of course, the veneer of our formal clothes and behavior did nothing to veil the fact that we had few skills and the collective confidence of a bowl of overcooked noodles. We were expected to "fake it until we made it", and eventually the rough wool of our nervous energy was spun into the refined yarn of *executive presence* as we developed experiential confidence demonstrated by a nascent ability to command the attention of a room of colleagues.

Gone are the days of watermarked paper resumés and pantyhose. With the exception of those applying to law firms, banks and some financial services organizations, most young professionals don't even own an interview suit. Many do not spellcheck their resumés, maintain eye contact or send messages of thanks. This is the new job marketplace and it can be tricky for those who aspire to be impactful leaders.

Over the years I've spoken with dozens of business leaders who have lamented the lack of *executive presence* and professionalism among their younger team members and job candidates. I've heard stories about texted resignations, terrible listening skills, shirked responsibilities, workout clothes as office attire and a general inability to verbally communicate without a plenitude of filler-words like *likes, umms, you-knows* and *ill-timed sorrys*. Sometimes the protagonists in these stories simply don't care, but more often than not, they are professionals who aspire to do great things in their careers but need guidance, direction and an emotive investment from a compassionate leader. This support is essential to fostering self-confidence in ambitious younger professionals. Before we can quantify just how valuable self-confidence is, we must first recognize its absence.

Not long ago I was working with a young professional who was about 5-6 years into his career. He was driven and enthusiastic about his job. He was also extremely frustrated with the lack of structure in his work environment. He felt a lot of pressure to do everything right and was afraid to admit when he needed help or training. He never received a formal job description and his direct supervisor was friendly but ill-equipped to provide him with thoughtful guidance. We discussed various scenarios where he and his team faced professional challenges and I asked him to provide me with examples of solutions he had come up with on his own. He was silent and reflective. He then asked me to clarify my question. Instead, I gave him a fictitious scenario in which I created a situation that required a pragmatic self-starter mentality. I asked him to share his ideas on possible solutions. He shared some random thoughts with me and then shrugged telling me he was fresh out of ideas.

I asked him why he didn't consider A, B or C and he responded that he held himself back out of fear of being a "burden". He explained that he did not feel he was competent enough to take charge of situations among his peers and that he feared being judged for "imposing his opinions and needs" on others. His candor was revealing. This story illustrates how the dearth of self-confidence among many 20 and 30-somethings birthed the myth of Millennial laziness and entitlement. It's not just Millennials, however. There are plenty of Gen X professionals that have greyer hair and bigger salaries, but still struggle mightily with knowing their value in the workplace and beyond. For those of us who aspire to leadership roles, addressing these insecurities is paramount to paving a path to impact.

SARA

Sara was on the path to partnership in a regional consulting firm. She was admired by colleagues for her hard work and dedication to the firm's clients. Sara was excited to take on a leadership position, but she was also incredibly anxious about what partnership would entail. Her introverted personality always lent itself to a *worker bee* mentality, where she'd be productive *behind the scenes*. She was raised to keep her head down and focus on the task at hand, with no encouragement to speak up and step out of her comfort zone. Intellectually, Sara knew she wanted to become partner so she could have an impact on her firm's cultural direction, hiring practices and approach with clients, but she struggled with *how* she would do it.

When she'd attend client meetings with partners, she always assumed the co-pilot role, only speaking up when invited to do so. And once all eyes were on her, her insecurities took over and she'd retreat, avoiding eye contact and sinking into her chair as she'd quietly share an idea or two. Sara's awkwardness stemmed from the fact that these meetings were attended by senior level professionals, all of whom had an average of 10 years' more experience than she. Her self-doubt inhibited any attempt at innovation and jeopardized her ability to have the impact she imagined for herself and her organization. She had conditioned herself to believe that somehow her ideas didn't merit the same consideration as her peers because she didn't think they would take her seriously. Sara saw her youth, experience level and gender as obstacles to taking *her seat at the table* and was unsure of how to get past feeling like an interloper in team meetings. She retained me to help her with these challenges so she could better position herself both to be invited to the partnership table *and* to help empower her so she could be impactful once she got there.

I helped Sara to think about her *holy trinity of WHY* and once she was clear on what she really cared about she was prepared to resolve what scared her. Once she clearly defined her principles and how they would positively impact those she worked with, suddenly her fears seemed trivial. When she quantified her value to her direct reports, management, clients and community, she endorsed herself as a qualified advocate for impact. As soon as Sara understood how her perspective, skills and insights would deliver significant results, her path to partnership was clear and she was able to deftly navigate it herself. Her newly minted confidence empowered her to take on more leadership responsibilities both within her firm and in the community, and in doing so she inspired several of her team members to do the same.

If you can relate to Sara, you're not alone. Most of us have felt like imposters in the workplace at one time or another, and many of us still find it challenging to approach some situations with confidence. To reach our goals we must develop the ability to negotiate difficult conversations and high-level decisions. We must demonstrate conviction and poise when soliciting the support or buy-in from others. But how can we do so if we are not skilled at articulating and conveying *why* our colleagues and clients should care about our efforts?

Exercise 4:

DEVELOPING EXECUTIVE PRESENCE

The 5-Step Process

- We must strive to understand the motivation of our audience (colleagues, direct reports, supervisors, prospects, clients, investors & referral sources
- We must own our WHY
- We must clearly define and effectively convey our value
- We must be conscious of how our message is delivered to ensure success. This includes tone of written and verbal communication, body language, eye contact, active listening & posing strategic questions
- We must also be aware of how our physical appearance (attire, grooming) might affect others' impressions of us to minimize distraction from our ideas

Chapter 5

Empowerment and Accountability

Several members of my family struggle with *Executive Functioning Disorder*, which affects their ability to analyze, plan/organize for and complete tasks in a timely and efficient manner. This means that our house is always buzzing with repeated directions, lots of last-minute scrambling and candidly, much frustration. It has taken years of practice, a lot of help from therapists, experts and schools for my husband and I to come to understand what we can and cannot reasonably expect from our children who struggle with managing a variety of tasks.

The challenges they face are not a sign of a lack of intelligence or interest, but instead a reflection of a difficulty with thinking strategically about how they will execute on and succeed at a task that is assigned to them. Even the smallest tasks like homework, cleaning their rooms or getting ready for school can be a struggle. As a mom, in addition to learning to cope with Executive Functioning Disorder, I've also learned a great deal about cognitive processing speed and managing the behavior of those with an attention deficit. The most difficult part about being a parent is intimately understanding your children's strengths and challenges in order to support them without impairing their ability to independently achieve. Similar to parenting, being in a leadership role requires us to take the time to understand differing abilities among those that we aspire to impact.

APATHY OR INABILITY?

A few years ago, I started to think about how learning differences and psychological organization affected professional accomplishments, and I had an epiphany during a client meeting. I had been working under the incorrect assumption that if a Rising Leader was properly motivated, they would, *of course*, be able to hold themselves accountable. For those of us who do not personally struggle with executive functioning, it can be extremely frustrating when we have colleagues or team members that struggle with keeping themselves on task. What I've begun to realize, however, is that follow-through and organized execution do not always follow commitment and motivation.

Some people fall short of seeing projects through to completion not because they lack passion or the desire to succeed, but because they require outside assistance with keeping their "eye on the ball" in order to move closer to reaching their goals. This means that those in leadership positions need to avoid rushing to judgement when working with a colleague who is having a difficult time staying on track. As leaders, we must first assess if our struggling colleague's true motivation is understood by both themselves and us. If we can check this box, then it may make sense to engage in a direct but sensitive dialogue about what might be standing in the way of success.

The roadblock may have nothing to do with someone's executive functioning ability. It may just be related to the fact that they are a more *in the box* thinker whose professional comfort zone is more reactive than proactive, and this is not necessarily a bad thing. If a team member possesses a number of strong and valuable skills, then the inability to reach the gold at the rainbow's end all on one's own is a challenge that may be managed through a number of different approaches such as mentoring, executive coaching and organized workplace peer support.

As Rising Leaders, we must consider educating ourselves on how to effectively manage people with organizational challenges. There are loads of brilliant and creative professionals who legitimately want to succeed but need external support and guidance to accompany them to the finish line. The most important thing to remember is to approach each situation with sensitivity, empathy, patience and positivity.

JENNIFER & DAVID

Jennifer was a terrific manager. In her firm, her devotion to her team was unmatched, and therefore she enjoyed a better rapport with her colleagues and less turnover than other departments. She loved what she did and felt totally in sync with *most* of her team, everyone except for David.

David was quiet and younger than most of his colleagues. He was recruited shortly after college and was good at following directions only when Jennifer explicitly laid them out. Once in a while, she would ask David to take on a task that required a certain level of independence as well as the ability to take some initiative, and he would routinely drop the ball. He would forget deadlines, neglect to follow up with Jennifer regarding his progress and refuse offers of help from his colleagues. She was becoming increasingly frustrated with David and was beginning to question whether or not he was the right fit for the firm.

Jennifer was a participant in a series of workshops I was facilitating on behalf of her firm, and David became the topic of one of our sessions. We were talking about accountability, and early in the conversation, the group – I along with them – held strong opinions about one's ability to hold themselves accountable. We initially agreed that this ability was *always* an indicator of passion, commitment and drive. Our opinions changed, however, once Jennifer told us about David. We began to question our beliefs once she repeatedly told us how dedicated and smart David appeared to be.

She raved about how his strong technical ability would shine through on every project he worked on. But then she began to lament the fact that she could not effectively delegate work to him without micromanaging the project. Her David stories reminded me of some of the challenges I faced at home with my children. I asked Jennifer if she had ever had any experience with learning differences. She told me that a few people in her own family struggled with attention problems and dyslexia. I asked her if David's behavior was similar to her family members, and after a moment of reflection, she nodded yes. I recommended that Jennifer sit down with David and reiterate to him how valuable he was to her team. I suggested that she present her concerns to him and then ask him directly if she, as his manager, could do anything differently to help him to be more successful.

At our workshop the following month, Jennifer's frown of frustration was replaced by a big smile. She told the group that she had a very successful meeting with David during which she helped him to feel valued and then asked him directly how she could help him to be more successful. She told us he was nervous at first, but then told her that he loved the work, but really struggled with time management.

He explained that even though he tried everything he could to stay organized, he continued to struggle with staying on task but was afraid to tell her for fear of losing his job.

This was a watershed moment for Jennifer. Suddenly she understood how to provide David with what he needed to succeed, thus paving her team's *path to impact*. They set up weekly meetings to discuss projects and share ideas on execution. They used apps designed for project management and consistently tracked his progress. Because David felt supported by Jennifer, he began to routinely approach her for help. This significantly improved her team's performance while at the same time helping David to focus on what he did best.

Of course, not everyone is David. There are plenty of people in the workforce who believe in doing the bare minimum and avoiding responsibility. As Rising Leaders, it falls to us to develop the skills we need to separate the slackers from those who are ambitious but in need of guidance and inspiration. If we all aspire take the time to understand each person we are responsible for, we can then play a critical role in boosting others' abilities and self-esteem, and this is what real impact is all about.

Chapter 6

Success

One of the most complicated words in our lexicon is *success*. Everyone talks about it. Everyone craves it. But few of us really understand what it means to *us*, let alone to our employers, staff, clients, communities and families. Once upon a time, professional success was always defined in terms of wealth. Today, financial well-being is still top of the list for most Rising Leaders, however, for most of us, money is not enough. Our motivation to go to work each day is directly tied to our desire to make a difference, to be a part of something bigger than ourselves, to resolve a problem, to create joy, to be impactful. Sadly, these ideas often do not become concrete realities because we don't take the time to detail how our efforts will translate to success both for ourselves and our organizations. Instead, we look to others to define what we should be doing, which subjects us to overwhelming external pressures and fleeting desires that only serve to distract us from the impact we wish to have.

PAST NORMS DO NOT DICTATE FUTURE REALITIES

I was working with an accounting firm to bridge the gap between the leadership styles of the younger managers and the more established senior folks at the partnership level. There was a palpable disconnect between the two groups and it posed a serious threat to the future sustainability of the organization. The partners had expressed frustration that their younger counterparts seemed uninterested in business development and growing their ledgers. As is the case in most professional services firms, building a significant book of business was a major criterion for earning the keys to the partnership kingdom. The senior leadership were alarmed by the struggle so many of their protégés seemed to have when they were expected to bring new clients into the firm. What the partners failed to realize was that the marketing malaise plaguing the younger managers stemmed from their indifference about the much-celebrated partnership track.

The group of young managers admitted to me that they were unsure of whether they coveted a seat at the partners' table or not. Their predecessors' paths were much more certain, as previous generations typically rode a conveyor belt to partnership, and they mistakenly expected that their younger hires would want – and do – the same. This group was made up of smart professionals who enjoyed their work, were passionate about helping their clients, prided themselves on their technical abilities and wanted to achieve a *work-life balance.* To them, this meant that they worked "normal" hours and were able to prioritize the quality of their personal lives over feeling enslaved to a grueling work schedule with little time to breathe. They understood the sacrifices required of them to qualify for partnership and they legitimately had no interest. The young managers were perfectly content in their current positions, managing client relationships and producing quality work, but because they were not empowered to honestly characterize what success looked like to *them,* the partners' plans for succession were forced to take a major detour.

Impactful leaders take the time to define both how *they* want to measure success and how *those they lead* want to succeed. This is not always easy to do. However, we must be empowered to be truthful and authentic about what success looks and feels like to us individually. Before we can effectively help others to realize their goals, we must be well-versed in what our personal motivations are to effectively measure our own major accomplishments.

SHARPIES AND CHAMPAGNE

This photo was taken in a client's office shortly after opening the doors of her own law practice.

If you are anything like me (and most of the Rising Leaders I work with) you set the bar *really* high for anything you want to accomplish. In fact, Rising Leaders are infamous for doing this. We set altitudinous goals and then place a sadistic amount pressure on ourselves to get everything done in an unreasonable amount of time. And when we actually hit our goals, there's no parade, no shower of confetti and no megaphone-wielding cheerleading squad. We set the bar high and we land on *said bar*. But instead of hanging out for a minute, having a glass of champagne and actually *acknowledging* our success, we break out the ladder and prepare to climb up to a higher bar. I did this for most of my career. If I was offered a particular job, it was taken in stride. When I landed a lucrative client, I calmly waited for my commission while I prospected for the next one. When I became partner and even CEO, it was business as usual, with absolutely nothing formally taking note of my efforts.

One day during my insurance career, I was having lunch with a friendly colleague and I was expressing some anxiety I felt about my largest client. I was questioning his loyalty and wondered whether he was satisfied with the work I had done for him because was not one to express gratitude. This, of course, preyed on the insecurity that plagued me at the time, and I wondered aloud if I stood to lose this important client. My friend asked if I had a legit reason to believe that the client would fire me. I didn't. I explained that the client had just renewed his policies with me for another year (generating new income), but since I didn't have a chance to personally connect with him when he did so, I wasn't sure he was totally pleased with the service our agency provided. In the cutthroat and over-commoditized business of insurance, clients are borrowed, never owned, of which I was keenly aware. He smiled and told me that the client's way of "thanking" me was to keep me as his agent for another year. He then asked me how I was going to "thank" myself by officially acknowledging my success.

I didn't know what to say. I never considered a sale a success, it was just how I earned my living. And I certainly didn't see repeat business as something to celebrate. For me, it just meant that my bills would likely get paid. My colleague explained that if I did not find some way to mark the occasion, it was like it never happened. If I never allowed myself to momentarily bask in the warm light of my accomplishments, I'd forever be running in a career hamster wheel pursuing a piece of cheese that would always be just out of reach. So, I started a new tradition in my house. I made sure to mark important successes, even those that seemed relatively small, with some kind of formal acknowledgement.

When StrategyHorse received its first check, I bought a bottle of my favorite champagne, shared it with my husband and wrote "First StrategyHorse check" along with the date on the empty bottle. The next bottle was to celebrate my retirement from the insurance business, and the next was marked for the 4-year anniversary of my consulting practice. My husband got into the "champagne campaign" as well, saving a few bottles to commemorate his becoming an investment advisor by passing several really difficult tests. As I write this book, the shelf in my office has 5 empty bottles of champagne with black marker all over the labels. I often glance over at my collection as I sit at my computer and it makes me smile.

The photo above was taken in a client's office. After working for years in less than ideal environments within large law firms, she decided to open her own practice. She was incredibly nervous about going out on her own, so I recommended that she open a bottle of champagne, celebrate her decision and save the bottle. She did, and it now sits prominently in the office of her super successful practice, reminding her every day that she made one of the best decisions of her life.

IMPACT VS. INFLUENCE

When I was 22, I landed my first sales job working for a large telecom company selling corporate long-distance contracts to businesses in the Washington, D.C. area. This was during the "telecom boom" of the mid-1990s, when businesses had a choice of phone service providers and competition was fierce. I knew little of the business world, which made me an attractive recruit for a company in need of green sales reps to follow their extreme sales tactics.

My boss John was only 25 himself and was in charge of an office of 18 sales reps, none of whom were over the age of 26. His job was to essentially bully us into closing deals. We were expected to walk unannounced into executives' offices, get them to sign a 3-year contract and abruptly leave their office as the ink was drying. To prepare us to become the revenue machines the company needed, we had to participate in a rigid sales training program that included videotaped role playing, stiff prospecting scripts and the memorization of passages from Dale Carnegie's famous book, *How to Win Friends and Influence People.* For those of you who haven't read it, this book has been a fixture on countless salespeople's bookshelves since 1936, and it promises to do 12 things for the reader, including:

- Increase one's popularity
- Help one to win people to his/her way of thinking

- Enable one to make friends quickly and easily

Like other sales training programs at the time, my company's approach had only one thing in its sights: closing deals. My boss had no interest in helping me to "win friends", but he certainly did everything he could to get me to exert our company's influence on the phone habits of D.C. executives. He had but one goal: do whatever you can to get the customer to do what *you* want them to do. My tenure at the telecom firm was short-lived, as I quickly burned out from the high-pressure environment in which daily insults were screamed at me for occasionally not hitting my sales quota. Perhaps this is why the word "influence" has never sat well with me. In my mind, to "influence" someone indicates an intent to manipulate them. My boss trained me to influence customers' buying decisions, even when my pitch was *not* in their best interest.

I was being paid to *influence* people to agree to a bad deal, and while I enjoyed my incentive-based compensation package, no amount of commission would have made this job more palatable. In the early days of my career, each time I accepted a new sales position with a company, I had to go through similarly aggressive training programs. In six years,

I went through four programs. Some of the sales trainers claimed to teach "needs based selling", but each regimen was just a more pronounced focus on asking robotic open-ended questions. No one ever taught us how to truly understand the motivation of our buyers...or more importantly, what would motivate them NOT to buy.

Eventually, I wanted to do more. I wanted to provide my clients with *value,* and I had no interest in *influencing* people in the way I was taught. It took me many years to understand how to genuinely connect with clients and referral sources about what they desired or feared, and the results were that my client base and network grew exponentially. Not only did I build lucrative businesses, but I was also graced with rewarding relationships with trusted colleagues and advisors. None of my success ever came from Carnegi-esque "popularity" or an ability to "win people to my way of thinking". Instead, it was powered by a genuine interest in providing transparency and value to my relationships, which created a footprint that I am extremely proud of.

Today, Millennials are targeted by companies with expansive "influencer marketing" campaigns. Social media accounts depicting celebrities using certain products and ubiquitous blogs of this "game-changer" or that "disruptor" flood our screens. It's no surprise that Rising Leaders that aspire to do great things are attracted to others' stories of doing great things themselves. The idea that positive energy and success is contagious is fantastic in theory, but reality dictates otherwise. After all, how can we expect that whatever steps those in the *influencer* spotlight took to realize their dreams will automatically work for us? Without a clear understanding of individual motivation and a healthy effort to quantify the impact we want to have, no number of "hacks" will cause success to magically materialize.

QUANTIFYING IMPACT

Being impactful at work and in the community is not just about *dreaming big*. We must take the time to visualize *how* we want to accomplish important things. As this concept can be fairly abstract and can easily overwhelm most of us, I've come up with a simplified method of laying out our plans for maximum effectiveness. It's called *The Impact Map*.

Exercise 5:

IMPACT MAP

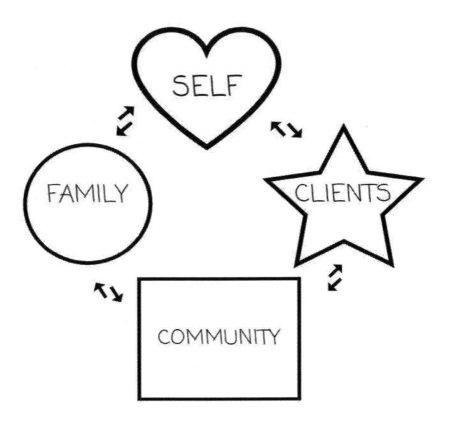

The exercise is based on the idea that if we carefully define how we'd like to benefit each one of these categories, our impact will increase ten-fold. If done correctly, we will construct a continuous circle of doing good, helping others, filling important needs and fostering innovation.

Here's an example of how it works:

SELF

If we are so focused on providing value to others that we lose sight of our own personal milestones, we will limit our ability to be an effective *vehicle of impact*. Let's say that we are interested in running a socially conscious business because we are committed to financially benefitting both ourselves and the community in which we live. We set ourselves up for success by reading books on the subject and speaking with known experts and peers who have successfully run companies based on a foundation of giving back to the community.

We take time to articulate *why* we want to do this, *how* we will accomplish this and *what* the outcome will be. In other words, we specifically define our role in hitting our own individual goals. Once we do this, we will then be able to understand how we will best impact our clients, family, friends and community.

FAMILY

Once we are clear about the impact we want to have for ourselves, we can then be mindful of the value we'd like to provide to others, turning our sights to how this vision will positively impact our family and those closest to us. Staying with the socially conscious business theme, if we lay out a straightforward plan including both our goals and a clear-cut path to execution, we will be able to substantially support our family's financial situation and the well-being of others concurrently. An additional benefit is the example that we are setting for the rest of the family, encouraging tomorrow's leaders to aspire to impactful lives themselves.

COMMUNITY

Because we've taken the time to carefully plan out *why* and *how* we'd like to be impactful with our business, we are able to channel funding to and create opportunities within the community as well. We will know exactly *where* we would like to make investments and *who* we want to benefit from our efforts. The economic investment both from direct funding and the creation of jobs will serve to strengthen the community, making it a more desirable place for us, our families, our neighbors and our clients.

CLIENTS

When we concentrate our energies on being a valuable resource to those that we serve, it's logical that we will have a lasting impact in the form of the solutions we provide. If we take the time to intimately understand our clients' needs and design our business around becoming indispensable to them, our efforts will positively impact those that patronize our organizations, the communities in which they do business and, in turn, their families.

A RISING TIDE LIFTS ALL BOATS

You'll notice that the connecting arrows in the diagram go in two directions. This illustrates how each category can – and should – mutually impact one another, provided intentions are clear and efforts adhere to the overall commitment to the *rising tide*. Vision combined with intentionality and responsibility will not only enhance everyone's contribution in the near term but will foster sustainable and shared improvements for years to come. The concept of *impact mapping* applies to the promotion of sound leadership practices as well as the establishment of a savvy and ROI-driven business development process.

BRIAN

Brian was a lifelong banker. Even though he was only 32 when I started to work with him, by that time he had worked in some capacity for a bank for over 16 years. His ascent from his first job as a teller in high school to becoming a regional vice president was a source of great pride for Brian.

Like many other professionals his age, Brian was a hard worker. His commitment to being a team player was unwavering, and because of this, he would often take on the workload usually allocated for 3 different people. His most recent employer was a large regional institution that hired him to support a huge effort to overhaul the bank's historically lackluster performance in the local community.

Never one to shy away from a challenge, Brian jumped in and rolled up his sleeves. The bank asked a lot of Brian and he was willing to make sacrifices, including working 12-14-hour days and missing family time on the weekends to venture into the office. What kept Brian going strong was his dream of contributing to the potential innovation of the business banking world. He spent years observing many flaws in the system and was driven to fix what was broken.

When he was recruited for the regional VP position, the hiring team liked his spunk and led Brian to believe that he would be empowered to enact real change both internally and with clients that craved a new way of doing things. Brian dove into his new job. He was excited about both the challenges and the opportunities of the uncharted waters he was about to enter. Fueled by adrenaline, coffee and a need to prove himself, Brian took on every task that was given to him. It didn't take long for him to feel like a hamster in a wheel. He was pouring energy into several projects at a time and had no idea if any of his efforts were successful.

Brian was always in improvement mode and he had retained me to help him remain accountable to his personal and professional goals. During one of our coaching sessions, he shared his frustration with the fact that he was unable to quantify the impact of all of his hard work. I suggested he keep a weekly diary to track his ideas, their execution and the outcome of his efforts. For Rising Leaders who are full of ambition, it's easy to experience burnout when you pour energy into your job and have no way of gauging success. An *Impact Diary* is a useful tool to manage efforts and ensure positive and quantifiable outcomes. Brian was religious about recording his efforts and the context of his progress, and his diary became an invaluable tool in the further development of his individual value proposition.

This tool is great for measuring impact and providing valuable feedback designed to help ambitious Rising Leaders channel their efforts in the most robust way. I recommend reviewing the entries on a monthly basis as well as every six months. The information collected will reveal much about both yourself and those working with (or against) you.

Exercise 6:

CREATING AN IMPACT DIARY

Head to Target or Walmart + pick up a ruled notebook (you can also do this on your computer or with an app, but I prefer good old pen and paper). Start by writing today's date at the top of the first page + title it "Week One".

Each week's entry will have four sections:

1) A new Suggestion/Recommendation/Idea you shared with colleagues, your team and/or your supervisor
2) To whom was it pitched + why?
3) Was your idea implemented? If so, was the objective reached? How long did it take? Who was responsible for its execution? If not, why? Where did the buck stop + how long did it take for the idea to die?
4) What is your current mindset this week + how did this week's events contribute to your mindset?

Chapter 7

Risk

To become impactful leaders, we must become intimately aware of our relationship with risk. We must understand the varying levels of threats that stem from the choices we make. It can be risky to be a leader. To have conviction about something and then back up our beliefs with bold actions can make us unpopular among our peers, and taking a stand exposes us to the possibility of offending others who do not share our opinions. The risks leaders face often come from the most seemingly benign sources, and if we do not learn to recognize and manage them, our *path to impact* will be destined to fail. Effective leaders take the time to understand their relationship with risk to ensure the efficacy of their efforts.

Your Box or Pandora's?

Pandora's Box is a Greek myth that has fascinated people for thousands of years. The story is about how the Greek god Zeus punished mankind because the mortal Prometheus stole fire from Mt. Olympus and gave it to humans without Zeus' consent. He created a beautiful woman called Pandora and the god Hermes presented her to Prometheus' brother to be his wife. Pandora was given a box that the gods directed her to never open. The box contained special gifts that tempted her on a daily basis. Eventually Pandora's great curiosity overcame her, and she opened the box, releasing terrible things on humankind. Once she saw the evil spirits pouring out of the box she tried to quickly close it, locking Hope, the only good thing placed there by Zeus, inside.

I believe that many of us think that stepping out of our own box is the equivalent to the opening of Pandora's box. We fear that our ambition will somehow expose us to dangerous risks that threaten whatever sense of security we believe ourselves to have. These perceived risks are as imaginary as the story of Pandora. The real risk is believing the myths we have created for and about ourselves and allowing it to derail our *path to impact.* In this chapter, we'll examine some of the legitimate risks to leading impactfully.

The Risk of Safety

As I noted earlier, the receipt of a steady paycheck can lull us into a dangerous sense of false security, one of the greatest impediments to impact. My friend Anna had worked in the online media field for over 20 years and was laid off four different times. Just after the fourth time she lost her job due to budget constraints, we were on the phone chatting about her situation. She was understandably worried about her family's financial future, but I also detected a tiny bit of relief in her voice. She had been working for a company where the mission was antithetical to what she believed in. Anna had always been a passionate advocate for the rights of working women, and her now ex-employer was a company that regularly exploited women through negative content posted on its platform. I asked her to tell me what she would do if money was not a factor. After a pause, she explained that she wanted to apply her skills to help amplify the voices of working women to address challenges that prevented them from realizing their dreams. Really good stuff.

Then I asked her if she had ever considered doing her own thing, either in a consulting capacity, or starting her own communications firm. She said no. Anna went on to explain that her family had relied on her "steady" income for quite some time. She said that they couldn't afford to take that kind of risk and that she needed to find something that was "safe". I suggested that she reflect upon how she felt each time she was let go. Was this the kind of "safety" she was looking for in her career? I asked her if she considered working at the pleasure of someone who answered to apathetic higher-ups who cared more about profit than progress "safe". There was a pause. I knew Anna was thinking about what I said. She eventually said no, followed by several rounds of *What would I do? How would I start? How would I make a living?* The adrenaline was kicking in. I advised Anna to apply her nervous energy towards a planning process. I recommended that she sit down and take the time to think through the *Holy Trinity of Self-Advocacy* so she could organize her thoughts, recognize what might be holding her back and most importantly, articulate what she really wanted to do.

During the weeks following the termination of her employment, Anna picked up a few freelance writing gigs to help pay the mortgage. She continued her job search, but her heart wasn't in it. Our conversation had sparked something within her. She developed a new entrepreneurial spirit and it was guiding her efforts. A few months later, Anna announced that she had opened her own consulting practice. Her focus was on helping businesses create better environments for working moms. It took about 6 months for Anna to rid her stomach of its resident butterflies, but during that time she channeled her nervous energy into intense business development efforts. Within the first month she defined her vision and was intentional about how to achieve the impact she desired. In the third month she was profitable and a year later she had three contractors working for her.

Of course, the entrepreneurial lifestyle is far from easy. And for those who lack vision, accountability, thick skin and loads of energy, it can be disastrous. How many of us allow ourselves to fear self-reliance over looking towards someone else to determine our worth? To be clear, not everyone is equipped to be a successful entrepreneur. Businesses need employees that crave predictability, and in exchange spend their days putting their employers' goals ahead of their own. But for those of us that want to engineer our own path to impact, we must be able to discern the difference between our perceived risk of failure and the risk of complacency.

The Risk of Not Being Relatable (or Vulnerable)

Andy was a skilled business developer. He was so successful that he was invited to become a partner at his firm, charged with overseeing the entire company's growth efforts. His affable charm and self-deprecating humor endeared him to both clients and employees. Because of Andy's significant contributions to the overall growth of the organization, his partners thought he was a natural when it came to training others to follow in his footsteps. The idea made sense in theory, but in reality, it was a different story.

He took various team members out with him to make client calls together, he made strategic introductions for them, he invested in technical training. No matter how diligent his efforts were, he saw little improvement in his team's ability to generate new opportunities. One of the greatest things about Andy was the rapport he built with his employees. They trusted him, respected him and genuinely liked him. Despite the strong relationship between he and his team, it wasn't enough to translate into legitimate revenue growth. We sat down together to discuss his challenges and he expressed his frustration. He felt that he had done all that he could to make his team into eager business developers and he wanted to retain me to support his efforts.

I asked Andy if he ever considered the fact that he might intimidate his team. He shook his head and told me that was impossible. He said that he'd gone out of his way to ensure that his people felt comfortable with him and that this was evidenced by all of the friendly chatter around the office as well as the many successful social gatherings they attended as a group. I reminded him that his team was familiar with "successful and seasoned Andy" and was not privy to "early career Andy" who took five years to land his first big client. They were unable to consider all that he had to do to arrive in his current position because they weren't around to see it. From the perspective of his employees, he had *always* had the golden touch when it came to growing the business. And regardless of how much time he invested in developing his team, none of them ever imagined they could generate business like he did. They put him on a pedestal and were unable to relate his experience to theirs. This detachment only served to derail Andy's efforts at building up his employees' confidence because most of them assumed they could never achieve the same success, and therefore chose not to try.

We tried an experiment. Andy started to share stories of the many stumblings of his early career with various members of his team. He told them about how he'd lost big deals, almost got fired, made a huge mistake on a client project and got kicked out of several offices when he was first starting out. Upon hearing these stories, most employees were incredulous. At first, it was difficult for them to see their "fearless leader" struggling in the same boat as they currently were. But as he started to incorporate his own learning experiences into his approach to training his people, he became more relatable. It was Andy's relatability that empowered his employees to take more risk. They began to push themselves out of their comfort zones to inch closer to reaching their business development goals. Once they were able to understand how Andy became the leader that he was, they could begin to envision—and execute— their own path to impact.

The Risk of Not Being Curious

I have no special talent, I am only passionately curious. – Albert Einstein

I am insatiably curious. Asking questions has not only led to the growth of my business, it has also helped me to be a better mother, wife, friend, daughter and mentor. I am a perpetual student and I try to derive value from experiencing failure and disappointment. For those of us who aspire to lead impactful lives, once we lose the ability to learn we begin to *manipulate* others instead of *inspire* them. We see this play out on a daily basis in the political world. So many crises we face stem from a dearth of those *qualified to lead.*

Too many people in power seek to *influence* others to support their own self-serving agenda. Instead, they should demonstrate to others how to embrace personal responsibility to deliver a positive impact. If we fail to admit what we don't know, we can't evolve. And if we don't evolve, we cannot hope to innovate. As Rising Leaders, it is our duty to foster innovation, and to do so we must follow the ABC Rule: **A**lways **B**e **C**urious.

The Risk of Chasing the Work-Life Balance Myth

As a mom of three who not only runs her own business but is married to someone who also runs his own business, our lives are far from *balanced*. I would describe our household as perpetual organized chaos. Like so many, I am often envious of families with clear counters, no mountain range of shoes on their floor and a perfect record for the timely return of all school forms that require a parent signature. And I've found that the more I long for such a lifestyle, the worse I feel. Every day I wrestle with being ok with our blessed mess because no matter how much effort I put towards achieving organizational perfection, I am always one dirty sock away from getting there.

Many of the young Rising Leaders that I work with find themselves feeling the same way. They struggle mightily with managing the demands of their work, the needs of their family and the overall big picture impact they want to have. Instead of taking a step back and re-visiting their *Holy Trinity of Self-Advocacy*, they forge ahead, as though there were some prize for exhausting oneself on behalf of others. While I do not fundamentally believe in the possibility of achieving *work-life Zen*, I do believe that if we have a clear picture of what's important to us and why, we will be able to be intentional in all that we do. If we are intentional then we can plan, and the very process of planning always alleviates panic. Even if our plans change (and they will – again and again and again), if we take the time to think about how each activity contributes to our path to impact, we will be able not only to lead others to do great things, but also exchange a great deal of guilt for well-deserved pride.

The Risk of Too Much YES

Saying NO is very scary for lots of folks. Many of us tend to think that if we utter this word the doors of opportunity will slam shut, we'll make mortal enemies of people we know, or we'll suffer from perpetual FOMO (fear of missing out). The weird thing is, the more we avoid the occasional necessary NO, the further we travel *away* from realizing our goals and having the impact we desire. Many of us are people-pleasers; we believe that that we become more and more popular every time we nod yes. What we don't realize is that appeased people may *appear* to sing our praises on the surface, but they rarely, *if ever*, respect our position. And this renders us totally ineffective as both colleagues and leaders.

I know a lot about NO. I believe that my three children are the world champions of *not* accepting NO. My husband and I have loads of experience with standing our NO ground. Believe it or not, on occasion, our children have actually confirmed what we were hoping to be true – that they appreciate the boundaries we set and that the rules they usually complain about make them feel safe and cared for. Additionally, whenever they whined about another child having privileges that they themselves were not given, once the initial emotional meltdown subsided they would actually criticize the excessive permissiveness of their classmates' parents. These infrequent and validating moments *almost* make up for all the gray hair.

In the worlds of management consulting, organizational development, industrial psychology and HR, the importance of providing a clear mission and structured professional development programs is the gospel. What often falls by the wayside, however, is how essential it is to create and enforce rules and policies to maintain a healthy and productive workplace culture. In other words, leadership's adoption of a reasonable NO policy once in a while and then sticking to proverbial guns. Much like children thrive in a structured environment where there are consequences for the choices they make, we, our teams, colleagues, managers and clients require a healthy dose of NO on a regular basis. To grow, we must be productive and intentional. If we are always distracted from where we should be concentrating our energies, we will never reach the ultimate YES.

This not only applies in office environments or within a family; accepting NOs is also essential to those of us who work for ourselves. Rejection and failure are two critical ingredients in the recipe for success and to be truly impactful we must believe that *the NO will always lead to the YES.*

WANT TO GROW? SAY NO.

I've had the fortune of working with some exceptional young professionals. Super-bright and eager, I've observed their unending enthusiasm to be both contagious and a health-hazard at the same time. Whether it's facilitating a board meeting or leading a strategic growth discussion, the most dynamic young participants all seem to share a stunning fear of saying "no". The general consensus is that taking on too much work will somehow satisfy cravings for an endless supply of pats on the back and *atta-boys*.

Unfortunately, it has been my experience that these overeager folks end up burning out due to perpetual job dissatisfaction and failed quests for the ever-evasive *work-life balance*. They lose their steam because their lack of focus and caffeine-fueled energy levels are not enough to achieve the successes they aspire to. Couple this with the fact that their managers are often spread too thin themselves to recognize these issues, and it's a recipe for disaster.

Great leaders understand the importance of setting boundaries, managing expectations and teaching others to do the same, and this requires a well-considered "no" once in a while. Contrary to popular belief, building a culture of "yes men and women" will *not* generate smart or sustainable growth. Instead, any progress that might be made will be dampened by high turnover and a risk to an organization's brand.

The Risk of Not Taking Ownership

Taking responsibility for one's decisions and choices is a big topic in our house. Every day my husband and I try to help our kids understand the consequences of shirking their responsibility and/or *passing the buck* to someone else. Candidly, it's one of the most difficult challenges of being a parent – or a leader of any kind. As leaders, we often feel as though we carry the weight of the world on our shoulders. I know I struggle mightily with this. To be effective and impactful, however, we must find ways in which we can empower others to take ownership of their role in solving challenges both at work, at home and in our communities.

SODA MACHINES AND LEADERSHIP

Katie and Erica worked in the same office and shared the same penchant for sugary caffeinated drinks. They both frequented the lunchroom vending machine a few times a week to feed their *Mountain Dew* craving. One day Katie walked down to the lunchroom with money in hand, excited to grab an icy cold can of her favorite soda. When she fed her $1.50 into the machine, nothing happened. She hit the change button, she banged on the machine, she repeatedly pressed the item number into the keypad. Nothing. No can of soda and no money. Katie was not happy. She shrugged her shoulders and headed back to her desk frustrated and undercaffeinated.

About an hour after the vending machine ate Katie's dollar, Erica headed to the lunchroom to grab a caffeine fix herself. She too fed her money into the machine with no results. After trying many of the same approaches that Katie had employed an hour earlier, she was left disappointed and thirsty, just like her colleague. Instead of just walking away in frustration, however, Erica taped a note to the machine warning her soda-drinking officemates of the glitch. She also walked down to the office manager who was charged with the vending machine maintenance and reported the problem, so a repair could be scheduled.

It's important to note that Katie and Erica were both managers with equal responsibility and at the same salary level. Even if the two professionals seemed the same "on paper" in terms of their skill sets and job descriptions, the vending machine incident illustrated a major difference in each woman's willingness to *own a problem* – the cornerstone of leadership. Erica's actions clearly reflected her ability to be impactful and Katie's did not. We've all encountered "Katies" who were unwilling to take personal responsibility in their personal and professional lives. I suppose they believe it to be easier to point fingers at someone else, or that they simply assume there will always be another person to clean up whatever mess they create or encounter.

Curious as to what some of the underlying reasons for this might be, I presented the Erica and Katie story to a young professional I was asked to coach. She was 26 and had about four years of work experience at the time. I asked her what she would do if the soda machine ate her money. She told me that she would have walked away from the machine and assumed that "someone in charge would have already be working on fixing the problem". I asked her if she would consider leaving a note on the machine or reporting the issue to the office manager. She said no. When I asked her why, she told me she "didn't want to seem pushy or cause a stir". This young woman's response totally surprised me as I personally wouldn't have made the connection between warning someone about a dollar-eating machine and being "pushy".

Her honest feedback made me realize something really important. The ability to take charge of a situation and own one's responsibility requires us to possess a relatively strong foundation of self-confidence and an understanding of the value we present to those around us. If these skills were not developed in us by our parents, we look to our workplace superiors to instill them in us. This realization evades many seasoned managers because they expect – and assume – that their employees will arrive on their first day pre-programmed with executive presence and enough confidence to run on auto-pilot. The fact is, this is rarely, *if ever*, the case. Younger professionals always need guidance and investment from their supervisors, even if they don't realize it themselves. A skilled leader anticipates this and takes the time to understand the individual needs of each team member, and then commits to providing tailored support to springboard their success.

I've found the "soda machine" question to be a useful tool in quickly identifying someone's willingness to take ownership of a situation. If their response illustrates their insecurity or avoidance of responsibility, it doesn't mean we should completely write someone off, however. Instead, it presents a unique opportunity to dig into why they wouldn't do something about the broken machine and help them through their challenges. Skilled managers and mentors understand their critical role in developing those that look up to them, and this is how we will create more impactful leaders and effect positive change in the workplace and beyond.

Chapter 8

Amplifying Impact

So far, I've shared ideas on how we can best focus our *individual* efforts to be most impactful, but why stop there? For those of us who seek opportunities to inspire others to create their *own paths to impact*, we must be thoughtful and intentional in our approach.

KOOL-AID, SAUSAGE AND BAD APPLES

What Flavor is Your Kool-Aid?

The phrase "drink the Kool-Aid" was coined in reference to the horrific 1978 Jonestown Massacre where 918 people died by drinking poisoned Kool-

Aid, as directed to do so by cult leader Jim Jones. Dark and morbid, I know.

Today, many of us use the phrase in a more positive way to describe an inclination to "buy in" to a school of thought. When I talk about how leadership drives smart growth in an organization, I frequently reference *Kool-Aid drinking* as a means of describing one's commitment to a brand, culture, mission or vision. For those of us charged with inspiring others to be impactful, we must first ensure that those we lead really understand *what* we are asking them to do, *why* we'd like them to do it and *how* their behavior will deliver their desired impact. We cannot safely assume that all members of a team intuit what they're supposed to do automatically. It is our responsibility as leaders to supply them with any and all information required for them to succeed.

Several years ago, I was retained by a large advisory firm to work with a select group of their most promising younger professionals. The firm was concerned that their present leadership was aging and that there were not enough of their younger counterparts to fill seats that were about to be vacated. They hired me to help cultivate critical business development and leadership skills within this group of promising professionals. During our first workshop together, I asked the group to define their employer's value proposition and to describe the company's branding. None of the participants could respond. Even though the average tenure of the group was 10 years and most of the participants had gone through numerous corporate training programs, not one of the professionals attending the workshop could articulate the *why* behind the services they provided. The radio silence response to my question was revelatory. No wonder the company was concerned about succession. How could any of these employees be genuinely interested in taking on leadership responsibilities if they couldn't comprehend exactly *what* they'd be leading?

I started talking about Kool-Aid. Cherry Kool-Aid, to be precise. I chose cherry because the company's branding colors were red and white. The senior leaders were pressuring this group of developing professionals to promote their flavor of Kool-Aid (corporate branding) without ever having tasted it *themselves*. How could anyone convince a person to try a "mystery drink" with no description of how it tastes or what the ingredients are? An uphill battle, to be sure.

This kind of thing happens all the time. Senior leaders expect their protégés to attract new clients but fail to provide them with a clear understanding of *how* and *why* they should reach them. It is always the responsibility of those at the top to both establish and effectively promote the corporate value proposition. Branding is more than just a logo, slick business cards or a cool color palette, however, frequently these things are the only means team members are provided with to grow their employers' bottom line. And the result is always a disenchanted group of talented professionals who often turn their frustration into a resignation. The key to engaging promising employees to become stakeholders in the future of an organization lies in developing a system for consistently distributing the same flavor of Kool-Aid, and here's what it looks like:

ABC Company's brand and culture is represented by orange Kool-Aid. The leadership has formally announced that they are all about orange and ensure that all managers enjoy this flavor and know how to prepare it for their employees' consumption. There are 5 steps to effective Kool-Aid distribution (brand ambassadorship):

RECRUITING

When a potential job candidate indicates interest in ABC Company, the recruiter provides them with a sample of orange Kool-Aid, which is a detailed description of company culture and mission. If the candidate likes the flavor she/he is invited for an interview.

INTERVIEW

During each interview the candidate is provided with another taste of orange Kool-Aid in the form of strategic questions and thoughtful interviewers. If they still like what they're tasting, a job offer is made.

ONBOARDING

When the new hire first joins the company, her/his direct supervisor meets with her/him to formally welcome them with a fresh glass of orange Kool-Aid as both a reminder of what they signed up for and a way to quell any concerns they may have about accepting the job. *It is during this critical part of the hiring process that a manager will either make or break their role as a leader.* A leader will take the time to sit down with their new hire and explain to them that even though the company Kool-Aid is orange, as long as they like the flavor, they can consume it however they prefer. A good manager will take it upon themselves to understand their employee's personal goals (the way they like their Kool-Aid prepared) and help to facilitate their success by preparing the sweet orange beverage mix according to their team members' individual preferences.

PERFORMANCE REVIEWS

Good leaders understand that their own performance is only as good as the performance of their team. The concept of the annual performance review is archaic, however, many organizations still use this model in managing their people. Managers must be predictably and consistently in touch with each member of their team throughout the year to ensure they are receiving the support they need and to gauge their employees' commitment to the orange Kool-Aid. If someone loses their taste for orange and begins to show a preference for cherry or grape instead, it may be time for them to move to another firm. Effective leaders understand that employee attrition is a reality and do all that they can to support their people even if a departure is imminent. In fact, some of the best sources of new business are ex-employees whose bosses handled their resignations in a kind and gracious manner.

PROFESSIONAL DEVELOPMENT

Investing in the professional development of employees is a critical component to the success of an organization. And if an employer is willing to commit time, money and energy to the training of its people, it should look for ways to incorporate orange Kool-Aid into the programming. This is especially important for business development training, executive coaching and mentoring. If a firm is to grow, its leaders should expect the staff to not only drink orange Kool-Aid, but to understand how to *successfully convince others to try it as well*. If leaders focus on developing internal brand ambassadors who are enthusiastic about promoting the orange Kool-Aid externally, the organization's marketing and recruitment efforts will improve significantly.

...Speaking of Kool Aid, What if We're Not Thirsty?

Several years ago, my husband became severely dehydrated after attending an all-day Formula One auto race in blistering July heat. When he returned home, he was weak and dizzy, and not thirsty at all. Losing one's sense of thirst is a strange symptom of extreme dehydration – and also why it is dangerous to forget to drink, especially when spending the day under the hot summer sun. This unfortunate experience taught our family a valuable lesson – to force ourselves to drink even when we don't feel like it.

I described how a good manager will remember to distribute Kool-Aid to their team on a consistent basis, but what happens if the staff's *thirst for engagement* is not anticipated by "dehydrated" leadership? This can present a big obstacle to smart growth for organizations with a multi-generational workforce. Baby Boomers, Gen X'ers and Millennials all have different levels of "thirst" and it is critical for impact-oriented leaders to understand and anticipate these differences.

BOOMERS: This group is perpetually dehydrated. Like my husband after a long day of roasting at the race, they don't feel thirsty themselves (don't anticipate the need for professional development or support from their superiors or peers). It does not occur to them that their colleagues may be extremely thirsty and relying on *them* to provide limitless Kool Aid.

GEN X: This group may not realize they are thirsty until someone offers them a drink. Once presented with a tempting beverage, they consume all the Kool-Aid (professional development, training, mentoring) they can get their hands on. X'ers will eventually advocate for their own hydration, unlike their Millennial peers.

> **MILLENNIAL:** These younger professionals are always thirsty. They seek proactive and continuous investment, support and mentoring — <u>not a trophy for effort</u>. The issue is, they struggle with pouring the Kool-Aid for themselves to quench their "thirst". Instead, they look to more seasoned leaders to anticipate their thirst and provide a never-ending fountain of Kool-Aid for their consumption.

Conscientious leaders will take the time to gauge people's thirst for support and guidance, provide the mentoring and investment Kool-Aid when needed, and, most importantly, will show younger team members *how to mix it themselves* for effective self-advocacy in sating their own thirst.

How is the Sausage Made?

We all know that profitability is a concern for business leaders in every industry. Those at the top of companies are presumably well-versed in how they make money, but what about everyone else on the payroll? If organizations want to grow smart, it falls upon their leaders to pull back the curtain and show their people *exactly* where the revenue comes from. When I was a kid, our family's favorite pizza topping was pepperoni. We loved the spicy, fatty salami so much that my mom would often buy sticks of the stuff to slice up and eat as an after-school snack. Not once did I ever read the label to understand what was *inside*, I just ate and enjoyed.

Fast forward to now. Due to health concerns, I've become quite adept at reading food ingredient lists and nutrition labels. I can tell you that pepperoni may make a random appearance in my house as an occasional treat, but now that I know about all the chemicals that go into highly processed meat products, it's never on the after-school snack menu for my kids. Historically, the business world has not totally embraced transparency in the determination of pricing. This was especially true in industries such as banking, insurance, legal services and accounting. Consumers saw these businesses as more of a necessity than a choice, and therefore offered their willing patronage with no expectation of understanding *how* these organizations made their money. This lack of transparency was not limited only to external customers but was also prevalent within the organizations themselves.

If you ask an insurance agent how a premium is determined, they will be hard-pressed to provide an accurate answer. If a lawyer is asked why their hourly rate is $350, there will likely be a pregnant pause followed by something about "market pricing". Clear as mud. Confusion is Kryptonite for smart growth because it leads one to feeling that they've lost control, which is guaranteed to erode trust. *And trust is, of course, everything.* It is not only imperative to landing quality clients but is also the key ingredient in a healthy and growth-oriented corporate culture. It falls upon tomorrow's leaders to ensure their teams understand the WHY behind what they do and HOW they make money, or they will not be committed to delivering WHAT they were hired to do in the first place.

Impactful leaders are dedicated to helping their people succeed and accept the fact that younger professionals will not willingly eat the sausage – or pepperoni – without knowing exactly what is in it. Not only will they not want to eat "mystery meat" themselves, they will be unable to convince others to try it unless they can properly articulate the contents. Leaders must educate themselves on what profitable business *really* looks like and commit to pulling this curtain back for everyone on their team.

The Precarious Path to Partnership

I absolutely love the navigation system in my car. Even though I have lived in the same community for close to 17 years, I still use my car's satellite system to get me around. It's my safety blanket. And it's totally worth the additional money we had to pay for both of our family cars to have in-dash systems. Even if I have an idea of where I am going, engaging the Nav system to help guide me gives me security and helps me to organize myself better so I can reach my destination in the most efficient way. Rising Leaders need the same kind of guidance in their careers. This is especially true for professionals that work for firms with a partnership group model such as accounting, engineering, consulting and legal practices.

It is almost unheard of for firms to provide explicit guidelines outlining the steps necessary to be offered an invitation to the partnership table. Promotions have always been subjective, as are compensation packages. Ambiguity is the norm, and like driving was before the advent of navigation systems, firm expectations have always been that ambitious professionals would somehow find their way to career success with limited guidance. This way of doing things no longer works, especially for the younger workforce who was raised in the era of in-dash navigation systems and mobile GPS apps. Because of technology, Millennials and younger Gen X'ers are accustomed to constant communication and need structured guidance to reach their goals. This is where the culture clash exists in the professional services space. Senior leadership prides themselves on having climbed the ladder the old-fashioned way, figuring things out as they went, and they expect their successors to do the same. The absence of clear expectations is the biggest threat to the future of the partnership model.

This lack of transparency has always benefited the leaders of these firms. The direction of the organization and its revenue model have traditionally been considered proprietary information reserved for partners' eyes only. This simply doesn't work for tomorrow's would-be leaders. To attract the necessary buy-in of younger leaders, senior partners must work to garner trust within the junior ranks. And Rising Leaders must effectively advocate for what they need to achieve their *personal definition of success*.

Too many in leadership positions expect their people to make the sacrifices necessary to arbitrarily demonstrate their commitment to the success of their firms, however, they are unwilling to provide concrete feedback about how to navigate the path to partnership. Without transparency, trust cannot exist. And without trust, a firm's life expectancy is finite. However, those aspiring to the leadership positions of the future cannot expect that their more seasoned colleagues will readily anticipate their need for structured guidance. They must be willing to lobby for what they need to be able to take the reins while looking out for the needs of their teams as well.

Rotten Apples

When it comes to bad leadership, a bad apple does not just spoil the bunch, *it can kill the whole tree.* Even if an organization has a vibrant workforce and a terrific culture, if there is a someone in a leadership position that exhibits toxic behavior, the whole company becomes a house of cards. Too often these bad players are kept around too long because they are *rainmakers,* or their supervisors or colleagues would prefer to turn a blind eye and avoid confrontation at all costs. This short-sighted approach can be a death sentence for a firm that aspires to grow.

It falls to Rising Leaders to do what they can to mitigate the damage to their teams' morale. This becomes a delicate dance, however, because while being sympathetic to employees' concerns is important, it is also unprofessional to undermine the perceived authority of someone in a supervisory capacity. This is where understanding the motivation of all parties involved is critical. Impact-oriented Rising Leaders must be able to acknowledge everyone's perspective and then take tactful and strategic steps to ensure that the objectives of all who are involved are aligned with the employer's vision.

THE GREG EFFECT

Even though Greg was in his early 40s, he was old-school. He had been a tax accountant for almost 20 years and was one of eight partners in his firm. He had one of the largest books of business at the firm so his frequently inappropriate behavior in the office was usually overlooked by his partners. He was sexist and grumpy and resented the fact that the younger folks on his team cared about trying to balance their personal and professional lives – especially during tax season.

Greg's partners knew him well. Behind closed doors they would confess their collective dislike for him, but no one had ever broached the subject of confronting him with their legitimate concerns. Instead, they would bite their tongues and watch the dollars from Greg's practice continue to roll in. The partners were increasingly worried about the fact that Greg's business made up such a large portion of their overall revenue and that their younger colleagues showed little to no interest in generating new client relationships themselves. It was risky for the firm, to say the least, and they retained me to work with their most promising younger professionals to help them focus on business development in an attempt to even out the revenue stream. Within minutes of meeting with the group of seven accountants, ranging from 28 to 38 years old, it was clear why they weren't interested in growing their practices. Greg's name came up several times during our initial conversation and anxious looks were exchanged around the room.

Each participant in the cohort was unwavering in their commitment to their profession. They glowed when sharing stories of helping clients and they sang one another's praises for being an exceptionally collaborative group. They were all thirsty for Kool-Aid, but Greg's behavior was poisoning the mix. After listening to the concerns of the group, I approached a few of the partners about Greg. I discreetly shared feedback about the general consensus on his presence in the firm. To my surprise, the partners were unfazed by anything I said and totally agreed with the group's opinions. I asked them what they were going to do about the negative effect Greg's lack of professionalism was having on the morale of their presumed successors. My question was met with silent shrugs and nervous glances at one another. The managing partner spoke up and said that they had tried to talk to him in the past and it hadn't gone well, that Greg was not receptive to any criticism.

Through their collective silence, the firm leaders were sending a mixed message to those being groomed to take over their business. They claimed to care about legacy and even hired me to help them invest in their people, yet they did nothing to keep Greg from derailing their plans. I explained that there was a possible mutiny in the making and that the future of their firm – and the vehicle funding their retirement – was at risk. In the end, none of the partners wanted to confront Greg. Within a year, only two of the seven young professionals remained at the firm. Many left just before tax season, leaving the partners (and remaining 2 younger managers) in a desperate hiring frenzy and with a larger workload.

The *Greg Effect* is found not only in accounting firms, but in law firms, engineering concerns, sales teams, consulting practices, non-profits, and the list goes on. Impactful leaders understand how to weigh the enduring soft dollars of employee morale, strength of culture and a keen interest in stewardship against the limited hard dollars generated by a toxic rainmaker.

Chapter 9

Break the Box, Set the Standard,

Be Impactful

PASSION, PRIDE OR PASSIVE AGGRESSION?

Effective leaders know that commercial enterprises, both for-profit and non-profit, cannot be democracies. If everyone on the payroll has an equal say about the goings-on, nothing will ever be accomplished. On the other hand, the same leaders understand how to skillfully engage their people so they experience professional satisfaction, while at the same time feeling secure in their employment because of the structured guidance put in place on their behalf.

Susan was the executive director of a regional non-profit. As is typical in this space, budgets were tight, and her staff were motivated by the work they were doing and not the limited compensation they received. The lean budget meant that everyone, including Susan, had a huge workload, and the office often felt like a hive full of very busy – and sometimes aggressive – bees. Susan was a maternalistic boss. She prided herself on how she doted on the members of her team. She felt appreciative of their hard work and believed in compensating for their low salaries by being excessively accommodating and rarely saying no. If an employee asked for a flexible schedule, Susan gave it to them without laying out any expectations. When the same employee started falling behind in their work, instead of addressing the concern in a productive way, she would send out a passive email asking them to "do better".

This approach didn't work because Susan never followed up with real consequences. And instead of making a necessary example out of a lackluster employee, she would allay the frustration of the other team members by being lenient with them, trying to appear "fair". In fact, Susan's efforts to be "fair" created systemic problems for the organization. Instead of efficiently delegating to her management team, she encouraged the entire staff to approach her directly with any and every concern they had. She kept employees on that were a drain on productivity. She wasted hours stroking egos and refereeing juvenile disagreements between her staff members. Her "open door policy" undermined any authority the management team should have had. The staff quietly resented Susan's management style because it did little to advance the mission of the organization. Her need to be liked instead of respected rendered ineffective even the efforts of her best people. If Susan had tempered her hunger for approval and focused on committing to the structure and guidance her team craved, she would have fostered an environment of collaboration and more streamlined productivity instead of one driven by insecurity.

GINA

Gina was a smart and sassy young professional. At 28, she was one of the promising "rising stars" of her company. She was curious, a quick learner and committed to her career. Gina also enjoyed being considered as "one of the guys" among her colleagues. Her company was known for its "work hard/play hard" culture and she loved the comfortable rapport she had built with both her peers and her direct supervisor. When her company retained me to help Gina and a group of her peers sharpen their business development and leadership skills, she quickly became my favorite because of her spunk and team mentality. She was the only woman in the group and seemed to be both respected and admired by her male colleagues, including those that were between 8-15 years her senior. The group and I would often meet in the late mornings and sometimes we would order in lunch.

One day we decided to make our session a working lunch and Gina was instrumental in arranging our catering order. As we enjoyed our sandwiches, we discussed the importance of defining everyone's individual value proposition and personal branding. We talked about how this group of greener professionals could engender trust and earn the respect of clients that were older and much more experienced than them. It was a lively discussion and the group seemed to come together and bond. At the end of the workshop, the table was covered with the remains of our lunch. And even though everyone had contributed to the mess, one person stood up from the table and began to clear the plates and deposit the trash – Gina. By the time Gina had cleared 85% of the table, her colleagues finally took the initiative to throw their stuff in the trash. But by then, the mess was already gone. Gina had succeeded in setting a dangerous example of how *not* to lead, especially for a female professional.

As soon as we were finished, everyone retreated back to their respective offices and I approached Gina to ask her if she would like some individualized feedback. She nodded eagerly, and I asked her why she took it upon herself to clean up the entire group's mess. She was visibly nervous and there was a bit of defensiveness in her voice. She explained to me that she was only trying to do "the right thing" by taking charge of the cleanup. She told me that her family had raised her to take the initiative in all cleaning efforts because it was the "polite thing to do". I understood where she was coming from because I was raised the same way. In my family, it was always the woman's role to prepare, serve and clean up after meals. The concern I had, however, was the message her behavior had sent to her *professional colleagues* in the *workplace*, a different environment than that of her family's table.

I knew her goals included assuming important leadership positions within the organization, so I explained to her the importance of leading by example. I told her that her taking the initiative in the cleanup effort was fine, however, the way in which she assumed *all* responsibility to clear the table set a precedent for her peers that could undermine even her best efforts at climbing the leadership ladder. Instead of tackling a menial task like clearing a table all by herself, a smart move would have been to engage several members of the team to take part. Had Gina rose to her feet after lunch, grabbed a plate and then asked three of her colleagues to lend a hand in the cleanup, she would have clearly established her role as a collaborative and thoughtful leader.

Believe it or not, it's simple stuff like this that can launch or sink an aspiring leader's *path to impact*. The workplace is quickly evolving, as are gender norms and the role of leadership. For Rising Leaders to be impactful, we must be keenly aware not only of our own ambitions, but also of how we are perceived by those we want to inspire.

Chapter 10

Mentoring

KAREN

I didn't understand what a mentor-mentee relationship looked like until I was in my mid-30s. It was then that I realized I had experienced my fair share of "anti-mentors" and felt it was time to seek guidance from people who knew way more than me. Everyone I met through my networking efforts was a source of information. I asked a lot of questions, solicited advice and sought opinions from professionals in every space. I surrounded myself with "mini-mentors" from whom I could gain insight and therefore develop my confidence.

Several years ago, while I was still in the insurance business, I attended a networking event geared towards professional women. Among the many accomplished women in the room, there was one person in particular that I was excited to meet. At the time, Karen was General Counsel for a local publicly traded company, and she enjoyed a stellar reputation for both her professional accomplishments and exceptional civic involvement. We shared a few friends in common, so I felt comfortable in approaching her and introducing myself. We chatted for a few minutes and exchanged cards. When I returned to my office, I did what I've always done after attending events, I sent her an email inviting her for coffee to continue our conversation. My agenda was simply to learn from her and maybe add her to my roster of "mini-mentors". Karen responded to my message immediately, however, it wasn't the response I was expecting.

> *Hi Wendy, thank you for your message. It was a pleasure meeting you as well. As I don't want to waste your time or mine, I wanted to let you know that we are all set for our personal insurance needs and the company's coverages are already well-managed.*

Her response took me off-guard. I quickly responded to clarify my intentions.

> *Karen, thank you for your message. I appreciate the fact that your insurance needs are all taken care of, as I'd be surprised if this was not the case. However, I wasn't reaching out to sell you insurance. Instead, I was hoping to spend a bit of time getting to know you as I've heard amazing things about you.*

Within 5 seconds of hitting the send button, I received a message back from Karen gushing about how she loved to make new friends and would be thrilled to grab coffee. When we finally got together, I asked Karen if she'd be willing to provide guidance and honest feedback about my career direction and some of the challenges I was facing. She was very enthusiastic about the opportunity to help me. Both her ear and advice were extremely valuable, and we continued to meet on a monthly basis. For the first year, our relationship remained somewhat formal. Karen was generous with her time and knowledge, and I felt privileged that she continued to commit time to our meetings.

Slowly, Karen started to reveal information about her own life. She was going through a transition in both her personal and professional life and I was eager to support her in any way I could. We continued to keep our monthly meetings on the calendar and our conversations changed over time. Our roles as mentor and mentee were blurred and we both took turns sharing challenges, ideas and advice every time we met. As we got to know each other better, we both became stakeholders in one another's success. Our relationship developed into a meaningful friendship based on this concept. What began as an interest in learning leadership and life skills from someone who I admired from afar, grew into an invaluable alliance based on a mutual love of learning, problem solving and living with purpose.

Asking Karen to mentor me played a pivotal role in helping me to understand and articulate my own individual value proposition. If I hadn't pursued inviting her for coffee and humbly asking for help, I'm not sure I'd be writing this book. Because I appreciate the value of being mentored, my commitment to mentoring others has been of the most rewarding things in my life. I am always asking people I meet if they have a mentor or would be interested in mentoring someone. Most of the time they say no, admitting they wouldn't know how to make it happen. Many younger professionals feel as though it would be an imposition to ask someone to be their mentor. Their insecurity, the very reason they need a mentor in the first place, is what prevents them from proactively seeking guidance from someone who is a few steps ahead of them in their own journey.

Being asked for guidance is the greatest compliment one can receive. Great leaders understand this and will usually consider it both an honor and a duty to share wisdom in order to amplify both their impact and the positive impact of others. There's no question that effective mentoring can play an invaluable role in a Rising Leader's personal and professional development. Like any worthwhile endeavor, creating something of value requires organization and intentionality.

Exercise 7:

FINDING A MENTOR

1) Assess where you are & where you'd like to be (The T-Chart is useful here). Then reflect upon the support you want from a mentor & prepare to articulate this

2) Think about your commitment level & overall goal for this relationship; Define what commitment means to you, think about how often you will communicate/meet & consider how you will measure success

2) "Shop" for a mentor by asking someone you admire if they'd be willing to work with you & then interview potential mentors to understand:
   a) How they define success & their road to get there
   b) How they handled adversity
   c) What commitment means to them
   d) Why they would want to mentor you & what they expect from the relationship
   e) What accountability looks like & how outcomes will be measured

4) Once you find the right fit, establish a formal agreement stating both of your objectives & expectations for the relationship

Once you've gone through your checklist and found the right person with whom to partner, turn it all around, become a mentor yourself and pay it forward!

Chapter 11

Build Your Bench

There are three things no one tells us when we aspire to entrepreneurial or leadership positions: 1) It's lonely at the top, 2) It can be lonelier with a partner or co-pilot if there is an absence of alignment and 3) Keeping one's own counsel is difficult when we're always guiding others. The best solution to all three challenges? Building a strong cabinet of smart, curious and optimistic folks that are stakeholders in our personal and professional success. These are the good people who will lend an ear, pat our backs and kick our asses to keep us on the path to impact.

These folks can appear organically through years' worth of strategic networking efforts, or intentionally by creating or joining a formal advisory or "study" group. Your cabinet should include anywhere between 3-8 stakeholders in your success and these people should provide you with the following:

- Recognition of your potential
- Help with articulating what you want
- Assistance with nudging you out of your comfort zone
- Accountability and regular questioning about how you are going about things to reinforce your commitment to yourself
- Reliability (they answer your calls, texts and emails and thoughtfully respond in a timely fashion)
- A circle of enthusiastic fans who personally share in your victories – and disappointments

Your professional cabinet is better suited for colleagues and "business friends" as opposed to your best friend or fraternity brother. You don't want someone who brings too much sentiment into their support of you and your efforts. There are times when your cabinet members have to get tough with you, ask you difficult questions and tell you things you don't necessarily want to hear. This is precisely what you should expect from your advisors, and you don't want to give them any reason not to be 100% straight with you at all times. Cultivating these relationships requires strategic thinking and a lot of time. I guarantee your efforts will yield big dividends, however, if you struggle with doing this for yourself, there are other options.

PEER ADVISORY GROUPS

Peer Advisory Groups are big business. These days, there is a spate of professionally created and facilitated groups of other leaders interested in coming together to learn, grow and thrive. If you are interested in surrounding yourself with qualified stakeholders in your impact journey and would prefer to have someone else populate and run your cabinet, go online and search for locally run peer advisory groups. There are international organizations that do this, as well as national franchises and locally run independent groups. When I was still in my early years working with my father, I was fortunate enough to join a family business-focused peer advisory group. It was designed for "future CEOs" and everyone involved was a son, son-in-law, or in my case, daughter, involved in a family-run business.

I participated in the group for over 5 years and I attribute 100% of my initial professional confidence to the interactions, discussions and overall support from this great group of guys. I'll never forget my very first meeting when I was formally introduced to the group. I had to present a bit about my business, my personal life and share with the group my biggest challenge.

I was very nervous, especially since I had been conditioned to keep any and all *dirty laundry* hidden deeply away. The facilitator expected me to be candid about my obstacles and I forced myself out of my comfort zone and shared with the group how I struggled mightily with self-confidence. After my mini-presentation, we went around the table and each of the 16 members commented. This was my first time meeting most of the members and they were all incredibly supportive and kind. There was one member who had a slew of Ivy League degrees and several successful businesses on his resume. When it was his turn to speak, he was incredulous that I doubted myself as much as I did and shared many supportive and sincere words about how he perceived me. The kind words from this successful guy coupled with the shared experience of the group were enough to spark a new belief in myself.

"STUDY" GROUPS

Years ago, a friend of mine said to me, "If you can't join them, lead them". This should be the anthem for anyone seeking their *path to impact*. Rising Leaders are sometimes the last ones picked for kickball. Many of us have had to work extremely hard to avail ourselves of opportunities.

For impact-oriented professionals that are interested in positioning themselves as resources for others, creating a small group of peers involved in complementary professions can be incredibly rewarding. The idea is to bring together professionals with a similar experience level who are interested in providing value to their clients in the form of a constant flow of knowledge and information. The group meets, shares *best practices*, examines challenges, and provides creative solutions to one another. The shared knowledge benefits everyone's respective efforts to be leaders in their field and the relaxed vibe of the group promotes organic business development and referrals. It's a brilliant model that I've both participated in, created and run on several different occasions over my career.

How to Create a Study Group

Let's say you are an estate planning attorney. Think about resources that could provide you with information that would be valuable to your clients. Make a list of these professions:

Example:
1) *Financial Advisor to manage money and provide financial advice*
2) *Banker to provide money management and trust services*
3) *Business Attorney to provide advice on contracts and general business matters*
4) *Home Healthcare Business owner to provide advice on supporting elderly and infirm clients*
5) *CPA/Tax Professional to give tax advice*
6) *Valuation Expert to provide business valuations for the estate planning process*

Once you have your list, start to reach out to your network and look for professionals to vet for the coveted positions in your new group. Figure out how often you want the group to meet and what each meeting's format will be (could involve guest speakers, case studies, etc.). Be sure that everyone in the group openly shares their expectations and commitment level, and I'd also recommend putting a confidentiality agreement in place as well.

The most important thing to remember is that this group is *not* a lead-exchange group. Relationships will develop based on the sharing of information and building of trust, and these will always lead to qualified business opportunities. These groups will often run their course after a couple of years, but sometimes they continue for decades, as long as members continue to derive value from their participation. This is why it is important to include professional peers who are all at the same stage in their careers. It's a simple and invaluable way to cultivate productive business relationships that can last for 30 years or more.

Chapter 12

Networking

"I HATE networking!"

I hear these words every day. Many people feel this way, even those that don't admit it. I'm an extrovert who's been networking for over 20 years, yet every time I arrive solo at an event, I have a flashback to the first day of 2nd grade. I imagine myself walking into the classroom, lunchbox in my hand, scanning the room for a friendly face to sit with. Grabbing my nametag as I arrive is enough to trigger the butterflies in my stomach, that is, until I spot a friendly face across the room. And then all is good in my networking world.

The word *networking* conjures up images of crowded events with stuffy people handing out business cards. It's an introvert's worst nightmare, and as I've already described, it's not that great for extroverts either. Unless you are a polished salesperson who has been trained for these situations, networking events are often disastrous. They leave little to show for the investment of money, time or energy, and that doesn't even include the hassle of driving around looking for parking. Whenever I ask a client or colleague what their reason for networking is, they always tell me it's to generate new business. No wonder they avoid these events, who wants to bear the intense pressure of having to sell oneself? Yuck! Looking for new opportunities at a crowded networking event is like searching for your future spouse at a crowded nightclub, not very likely to happen. But because becoming an effective networker is a practice that is essential to a Rising Leader's repertoire, we must understand that our success is all in the approach.

Networking is learning

There is a simple way to remove the anxiety from and exponentially succeed at networking: *Look to Learn*. If we try to learn something new from each person we connect with, we will not only grow our knowledge base, but also engender trust, discover ways to provide value and maybe even have some fun. Leaders should always be learning, and there's no better way to do this than to mingle with potential referral sources, grab coffee with a successful and generous colleague or exchange ideas with a new contact via social media. The best part? No selling involved. In fact, if we really embrace this approach, we actually end up promoting the impact we want to have without realizing we're doing it. It's all about engaging people to support your *path to impact* by asking them for advice, guidance, ideas and help.

The single most effective method I've found for building valuable relationships is to approach each new connection with the powerful combo of curiosity, enthusiasm and humility. Every leadership opportunity I've had the fortune to participate in has come from this idea. When I started my consulting practice, I set out to collect as much information as possible about ways in which I could provide value to the business community. I set up a slew of coffee meetings with people whose experience could contribute to the development of my brand and I asked for their opinions. I enjoyed many lively conversations and learned so much not only about how to best position my business, but also about potential roadblocks, the marketing process and where I needed to further invest in my own professional development. I continue to employ this technique as I concentrate on new ways to be impactful. I am always open to suggestions, ideas and opportunities and this has been the best way to ensure that I provide continuous value to my clients, colleagues and community.

Find what fits

LAURIE

When I first met one of my favorite clients, Laurie, she asked me to help her double her business. Then, in the next breath, she announced that she would not be attending any networking events and was unwilling to consider posting on social media…and that I "shouldn't even try to get her to do these things." I told her that I understood her concerns and would not force her to do anything she was not comfortable doing. My response surprised her, as she was sure I would force her to follow some hackneyed prescription for business development success.

I explained that successful networking had to be tailored to everyone's individual strengths and comfort levels. I told her that if she hated attending events, it didn't make sense for her to go. Our work was about figuring out what was going to strategically and efficiently grow *her* practice, not to follow some generic protocol that didn't make sense. Before we discussed how she was going to hit her goals, we spent time articulating her personal and professional mission and defining her brand. Once Laurie felt confident and excited about what she stood for, we discussed who would most benefit from working with her. This was an important and challenging conversation because at the time she was working in an environment that fanned the flames of her insecurity on a daily basis.

Eventually Laurie developed a clear picture in her mind of who she wanted to work with and why, and her confidence grew. She felt a bit better about "putting herself out there" in a networking capacity. The strategy we used to cultivate new relationships was to schedule one-on-one coffee meetings and avoid the events that caused Laurie so much grief. The first few people she invited to coffee were "low hanging fruit" – current clients and professional colleagues. These were the perfect folks for Laurie to practice her networking skills with because they already knew her and were supportive of what she was doing.

She prepared for every meeting by envisioning a projected outcome, so the conversation was both enjoyable and productive. The best thing Laurie did in these meetings was to ask for help. At first, she was nervous about being judged for soliciting feedback, but once she got past this and asked various fans of her work for their ideas on how to become more successful, she was blown away by their willingness to help. The positive feedback in turn helped Laurie to grow her self-confidence and created ownership in her own individual value proposition.

Within a year, Laurie tripled her book of business, became a partner in her firm and developed a significant thought leadership following on LinkedIn. During our first meeting I bet her that she would call me a year after working together and invite *me* to an event. Sure enough, about a year after we first started working together, Laurie called me and invited me to a women's networking event (still a little joke between us). Four years later, I helped her to open her own business. From day one, she was profitable and positioned for exponential growth. She was able to do all of this because she was not only sure of what, how and *why* she brings value to her network, but also because she is dedicated to impacting others in a decidedly positive way. This focus has propelled her to hang out her own shingle, hire and develop committed team members, take on leadership positions in professional and social communities and generously share advice with other professionals that aspire to be impactful themselves.

Rising Leaders must be prepared to continuously cultivate strategic and rewarding relationships. We should focus on *curating* valuable networks of solid resources instead of arbitrarily collecting names and business cards. If we approach each networking opportunity with a curious mind and a generous spirit, there is no limit to how successful we will be.

Reach outside of your box

I have successfully used LinkedIn to connect with all sorts of amazing people from around the globe. The vast majority of these contacts were strangers when I invited them to connect. Many Rising Leaders hesitate to accept a connection request from someone they don't know. This is a huge mistake. I'm not saying we should connect with anyone and everyone with no strategy whatsoever. Instead, I am suggesting that there is great value in "meeting" someone with similar interests, shared contacts, or a complementary *path to impact*.

But it's not just about *accepting* invitations from people you don't know, it's just as critical to consider *inviting* people you don't know to connect to create a meaningful social media footprint. There is no reason to fear sending a "blind invitation". The whole point of LinkedIn is to cultivate relationships, and "meeting" someone on the site or app can lead to valuable opportunities. Through the strategic growth of my LinkedIn network, I've been able to connect with inspiring leaders from around the world, and this has been invaluable to my professional development and my ability to create a platform to help Rising Leaders be more successful.

The same practice applies to in-person networking as well. "Unusual suspects", as I like to call them, can play a very important role in our professional development. These are people that we would not ordinarily expect to be our teachers. Any opportunity to learn about different perspectives as well as what motivates others provides us with the skills we need to be impactful. So, the next time you receive an invitation to connect on LinkedIn from someone you don't know, take a moment to read through their profile and see if you can find something of interest in their experience, interests and network. Also remember that once you are connected to them, you are also connected to their entire network, which can be a useful tool for amplifying your impact as an effective leader.

Chapter 13

Creating Your Path

If we are truly committed to inspiring others to feel good, do good and be good, we must dedicate ourselves to a lifelong journey of personal and professional growth. If we are to be successful, we have to be conscious of the restrictions being placed upon us by both ourselves and those around us. As long as we assume leadership roles, there will always be the proverbial box that we feel tempted to fit ourselves into. No matter where our lives take us or what situations we find ourselves in, we will be genuinely impactful only if we remain *aware*. To be able to plan for and navigate our individual *paths to impact* we must be equally mindful of what we care about and what we fear, as well as be cognizant of what drives the behavior of those around us.

Before we set out to do great things, we need to check in with ourselves. We will never be effective if we're always trying to fulfill someone else's expectations of us. If we dedicate all our energy to the pursuit of lofty goals determined by our peers or supervisors, our efforts will not be driven by our own sincere motivations and our intended impact will be diminished. Remarkable leadership is not about power or the inflation of one's ego. It's also not about satisfying our desire to be needed by positioning ourselves as wet nurses to the world.

Leading others in an impactful way requires us to never stop seeking ways in which we can provide value to anyone and everyone we meet, while remaining vigilant about staying true to ourselves. If we are successful at identifying and executing on opportunities to deliver value, we can then inspire others to do the same...and so on. Intuitiveness, empathy and intentionality are all important aspects to creating – and mastering – the *path to impact*.

So, what does your path look like? The first step to figuring out how you'll get to where you want to be is to start small. Think about little ways in which you can improve your situation as well as that of others around you. Take the time to reflect on what's most meaningful to you and don't hesitate to ask others what's important to them and why.

The best way to figure out how we can provide value to others is to simply ask them the BIG question: *How can I help?* Impactful leaders are unafraid to *put themselves out there* and be direct when it comes to identifying which dots to connect and the most effective way to do so. Never assume that anyone is too successful, confident, savvy or educated to need assistance. We can all use some help at one, if not many, times in our lives. The leaders that understand this and uniformly position themselves to share ideas (even when it feels awkward to do so) are the ones that will have the most impact. And this is how we become and create stakeholders in the continuous improvement of our workplaces and communities. Leading impactfully requires us to always keep our destination in mind and be sure to recognize each lesson learned along the way.

What does your path to impact look like and where will it lead you and those you wish to inspire?

45705491R00113

Made in the USA
Middletown, DE
19 May 2019